Kurdish Grammar

ڕێزمانی کوردی

SORANI Reference Book

Murat Baran

www.serkeftin.com/en

Copyright © Murat Baran

First edition 2021 Hewlêr

ISBN 9798455167294

Amazon Publishing
Cover picture: Olga Guchek

Preface

You want to learn **SORANI**? **Kurdish Grammar** ڕێزمانی کوردی makes it quite simple for you. It is directed at anyone who would like to learn the Sorani language – whether as a holiday-goer, culture- or language enthusiast, partner, student, or employee.

The overview tables for grammar and important verbs help to learn quickly and easily – with or without prior knowledge. This in addition to conjugation formulas and many examples gives you the opportunity to actively learn Sorani and spare you from longwinded, boring explanatory texts! You can use this book as a resource for the first steps and whenever you get stuck.

Kurdish languages (Gorani, Kurmanji, Sorani, Southern Kurdish and Zazaki) belong to the Iranian languages of the Indo-European language family. The book **Kurdish Grammar** ڕێزمانی کوردی is written in Sorani – this is the second most spoken language by Kurds and is mainly spoken in Iran and Iraq. In the latter, it is the second official language. Additionally, many people in the U.S. and in European countries like Germany, France and the UK speak Sorani.

A special thanks to *Qendîl Şeyxbizînî & Hemn Majeed* for their continued support in creating this book.

 This symbol indicates that the related text can be found as audio file. The audio file is also available on **www.serkeftin.com**

Murat Baran
Hewlêr, 2021

CONTENTS

Peculiarities of the Sorani Language 5
The Kurdish (Sorani) Alphabet 7
Peculiarities of the Sorani Alphabet 8
THE PRONOUNS 10
    The Personal Pronouns 10
    Possessive pronouns & suffixes 11
    Interrogative pronouns 11
    The Possesive Suffixes with the Pronoun هەموو 12
    The Demonstrative Pronouns 12
    The Reflexive Pronoun 13
    The Reciprocal Pronoun 13
    Diminutive suffixes 14
    Declension of nouns 14
    The verb "to be" in present tense 17
    The verb "to be" in past tense 17
THE PRESENT TENSE 18
    Present Progressive & Simple Present Tense 18
    Pronominal Objects in the Present Tense 23
    The Imperative 24
    نییه / هەیه 25
    The Modal Verbs 25
    The Subjunctive with Modal Verbs 27
THE PAST TENSES 29
    The Simple Past Tense 29

CONTENTS

Comparison of Present and Past tenses 35
The Past Progressive Tense 36
The Pluperfect Tense 42
The Present Perfect Tense 49

THE FUTURE TENSE 56

THE SUBJUNCTIVE 57

The Subjunctive (Present Tense) 57
The Subjunctive (Conditional perfect) 58
The Subjunctive (Pluperfect Tense) 62
Conditional Clauses 65
The Irrealis (Past tenses) 65
The Subjunctive with بـ 68

THE PASSIVE VOICE 69

In the Present Tense 69
In the Simple Past Tense 70
In the Past Progressive Tense 71
In the Present Perfect Tense 72
In the Pluperfect Tense 73

THE ADVERBS 74

1. The Most Common Temporal Adverbs 74
2. The Most Common Modal Adverbs 75
3. The Most Common Local Adverbs 76

PREPOSITIONS AND CIRCUMPOSITIONS 77

THE ADJECTIVES 78

1. Adjective as a Modifier 78
2. Adjective as an Adverb 78
3. Adjective as a Predicate with "to be" 79

CONTENTS

4. Formation of Adjectives from Nouns 79
5. Formation of Adjectives from Verbs (Participle) 79
6. Substantiation of adjectives 80
7. Comparative 80

CONJUNCTIONS AND SUBORDINATE CLAUSES 81

Conjunctions in Sorani 81
Subordinate Clauses in Sorani 83

STRUCTURE OF THE SORANI VERBS 85

The Simple Verbs 85
The Compound Verbs 85
The Separable Compound Verbs 86
The Separable Verbs 87

THE NUMBERS 88

Cardinal Numbers 88
Ordinal numbers & Fractions 89
Writing of the date 89

VERB STEMS 90

The Abbreviations 93

Peculiarities of the Sorani Language

- A personal pronoun is not obligatory to build a sentence. The personal suffix of the verb is sufficient.

  <u>e.g.:</u> من دەبینم → I see.

  دەبینم. → I see.

- The word order for positive & interrogative sentences does not differ. Question words such as ناخۆ، وەئە، ئایا، ڕێئە etc. (no meaning of their own) can be used, but it's not obligatory.

  تۆ دەچیت. → You go.

  ئایا تۆ دەچیت؟ *or* تۆ دەچیت؟ → Do you **go**?

- In Sorani there is no separate conjugation for "Simple present tense", "Present progressive tense" and "Future tense".
  For an exact differentiation, you need to use a time word such as *now, tomorrow, later, next year* etc.

  <u>e.g.:</u> دەبینم → I see   دەچم → I go/I'm going.

  دەبینم → I will see   دەچم → I will go

  ئێستا دەچم → I'm going **now**

  دواڕۆژ دەچم → I will go **tomorrow**

- The **word order** in Sorani:

  Subject + Object + **Verb**.

  من ئاو دەخۆمەوە. → **I drink** water.

  - with verbs that indicate a direction of movement:

  Subject + **Verb** + Object. or **Subject** + <u>Object</u>+ **Verb**.

  من دەچم بۆ لەندەن → **I go** to <u>London</u>. → من بۆ <u>لەندەن</u> دەچم

  Subject + <u>Object</u> + **Verb** + Object.

  من ئاو دەدەمە تۆ → **I give** you <u>water</u>.

Peculiarities of the Sorani Language

- with Modal verbs:

Subject + Modal verb + Object + Verb.

من دەتوانم ئاو **بخۆمەوە**. → I can drink <u>water</u>.

من دەمەوێت ئاو **بخۆمەوە**. → I want to drink <u>water</u>.

دەبێ من ئاو **بخۆمەوە** → I must drink <u>water</u>.

- **Verbs can be nominalized** with their infinitive form.

<u>e.g.</u>: خواردن – to eat

خواردن – food → خواردنم – my food

- In some regions of Kurdistan **d-** and **-t** letters are neglected.

<u>e.g.</u>: من دەمەوێت – I want. دەبێت من بڕۆم – I must go.

من ئەمەوێ – I want. دەبێ من بڕۆم – I must go.

تۆ چۆنیت؟ – How are you? → تۆ چۆنی؟ – How are yoou?

<u>Standard</u>: لە دڵمدا → in my heart

<u>Slemani</u>: لە دڵما → in my heart

- Comparison of some regional sentences:

دەچم بۆ لەندەن. → I *go to* London.

دەچمە لەندەن. → I *go to* London.

- In Sorani there are three ways to express a possessive:

ناو → name, من → my, م - (possessive ending equal to **my**)

1- ناوی من 2- ناوم 3- ناوم من → **my** name

The Kurdish Alphabet

initial	medial	final	isol.	IPA	Sorani	English
ئا	ـا	ـا	ا	[a]	ئاو (water)	father
بـ	ـبـ	ـب	ب	[b]	باران (rain)	buy
جـ	ـجـ	ـج	ج	[dʒ]	جوان (beautiful)	judge
چـ	ـچـ	ـچ	چ	[tʃ]	چاو (eye)	child
د	ـد	ـد	د	[d]	دەست (hand)	date
ئە	ـە	ـە	ە	[æ]	ئەگەر (if)	cat
ئێـ	ـێـ	ـێ	ێ	[e]	ئێستا (now)	lake
فـ	ـفـ	ـف	ف	[f]	فەرهەنگ (dictionary)	friend
گـ	ـگـ	ـگ	گ	[g]	گۆرانی (song)	guest
هـ	ـهـ	ـه	ه	[h]	هاوڕێ (friend)	house
حـ	ـحـ	ـح	ح	[ħ]	حەوت (seven)	Arabic Ḥā'
ئیـ	ـیـ	ـی	ی	[i]	ئیش (job)	meet
ژ	ـژ	ـژ	ژ	[ʒ]	ژن (woman)	visual
کـ	ـکـ	ـک	ک	[k]	کورد (Kurd)	cat
لـ	ـلـ	ـل	ل	[l]	لەش (body)	life
ڵـ	ـڵـ	ـڵ	ڵ	[ɫ]	گوڵ (rose)	similar like all
مـ	ـمـ	ـم	م	[m]	ماسی (fish)	man
نـ	ـنـ	ـن	ن	[n]	نان (bread)	no
ئۆ	ـۆ	ـۆ	ۆ	[o]	تۆ (you)	note
پـ	ـپـ	ـپ	پ	[p]	پەرتووک (book)	park
قـ	ـقـ	ـق	ق	[q]	قسە (word)	Arabic Qaf
ر	ـر	ـر	ر	[r]	فەرمان (order)	ride

Peculiarities of the Sorani Alphabet

initial	medial	final	isol.	IPA	Sorani	English
ڕ	ڕ	ڕ	ڕ	[r]	ڕەنگ (color)	Spanish **r**
س	س	س	س	[s]	سێو (apple)	**s**ea
ش	ش	ش	ش	[ʃ]	شەقام (street)	**sh**ape
ت	ت	ت	ت	[t]	تەمەن (age)	**t**ea
ئو	و	و	و	[ʊ]	کور (son)	p**u**t
ئوو	وو	وو	وو	[u]	دوور (far)	c**oo**l
ڤ	ڤ	ڤ	ڤ	[v]	ڤیدیۆ (video)	**v**ast
و	و	و	و	[w]	وەرزش (sport)	**w**est
خ	خ	خ	خ	[x]	خەو (sleep)	German **ch**
غ	غ	غ	غ	[ɣ]	غەم (worry)	Arabic **Ghayn**
ی	ی	ی	ی	[j]	یەک (one)	**y**ellow
ز	ز	ز	ز	[z]	زمان (language)	**z**ero
ع	ع	ع	ع	[ʕ]	عەرەب (Arab)	Arabic **'Ain**

Sorani has a digraph خو [xw] that occurs frequently.
e.g.: خواردن (to eat), خوێندن (to study)

Peculiarities of the Sorani Alphabet

- All words beginning with a vowel receives the symbol ئ at the beginning.

  e.g.: ا [a] → ئازادی [azadi] *(freedom)*

  ئ [e] → ئێستا [esta] *(now)*

- The letter ڵ [ɫ] never occurs at the beginning of a word.

- Normally words begin on a hard ڕ [r], not on a soft ر [r].

Peculiarities of the Sorani Alphabet

- Normally, a letter is written together with the letter that follows it. The following consonants are exceptions:

  د ، ژ ، ڕ ، ر ، و ، ز

  e.g.: دوو ، رمانفه ، ڕۆژ ، وڵات ، زۆر

- The remaining consonants are written together with the letters that follow them: ب، ج، چ، ف، گ، ه، ح، ک، ل، ڵ م، ن، پ، ق، س، ش ، ت، ث، خ، غ، ی ، ع

  باران، جوان، چوار، فرمێسک، گوڵ، وتحه، کور، لاق، لامپه، مێر، نان، پۆر، قاز، وزسه، شار، تۆ، ڕووسڨه، خاڵ، غار، کیه، بڕهعه

- The vowels ا [a] and ە [æ] are not written together with the letters that follow them.

  e.g.: ئەو، ئاو

- In Sorani the vowels و [ʊ] and وو [u] are phonetically very similar, so و is often neglected in everyday life:

  پەرتووک (book) → پەرتوک   خانوو (house) → خانو

  ئارەزوو (wish) → ئارەزو

- The letters [i] and [j] are written with the same symbol ی.

- The letters [ʊ] and [w] are written with the same symbol و.

- In Sorani there are two **buffer consonants** (-ی-, -و-). These separate vowels in order to make words easier to pronounce.

  e.g.: خانوو (house), خانووەکەم (my house), to shorten a و is neglected → خانوەکەم

  مامۆستایان (teachers (Plural))

THE PRONOUNS

The Personal Pronouns

There are six pronouns in Sorani which are used as *subject* and *object pronouns* as well as *possessive adjectives*.

Subject case		Personal ending („to be")		
من	I	م	→	am
تۆ	you	یت or ی	→	are
ئەو	he/she/it	ە / ات - ێت	→	is
ئێمە	we	ین	→	are
ئێوە	you	ن	→	are
ئەوان	they	ن	→	are

The letter ت is often neglected in daily life. ات - ێت are used in a verb conjugation not after a noun or an adjective.

e.g.: ئەمە باشە/سێوە *(This is good /apple)*

ئەو دەبینێت *(He sees)*

Object case & Possessive adjectives		Possessive pronouns	
من	me, my	هی من	mine
تۆ	you, your	هی تۆ	your
ئەو	him - it / her – it his, its, her	هی ئەو	his/her
ئێمە	us, our	هی ئێمە	ours
ئێوە	you, your	هی ئێوە	yours
ئەوان	them, their	هی ئەوان	theirs

THE PRONOUNS | 11

The Possessive Suffixes

If some wants to express of possession of something a special suffix is added to word.

Sorani	English	Example (ناو : *name*)
م	my	ناوم (my name)
ت	your	ناوت (your name)
ی	his - its	ناوی (his name)
ی	her - its	ناوی (her name)
مان	our	ناومان (our name)
تان	your	ناوتان (your name)
یان	their	ناویان (their name)

Alternative Form: ناوی من = من ناوم = **my** name

The Interrogative Pronouns

چۆن؟	How?	تۆ چۆنیت؟	How are you?
چەند؟	How many?	تۆ چەند ساڵیت؟	How old are you?
چەند؟	How much?	ئەمە بە چەندە؟	How much is this?
چی؟	What?	ناوت چییە؟	What is your name?
بۆ چی؟	Why?	بۆ چی دەچیت؟	Why are you going?
لە کوێ؟	Where?	ئێستا لە کوێی؟	Where are you now?
کوێ؟	Where from?	تۆ خەڵکی کوێی؟	Where are you from?
کێ؟	Who?	تۆ کێی؟	Who are you?
کەی؟/کەیی؟	When?	کەی دەڕۆی؟	When are you going?
هەتا کەی؟	How long?	هەتا کەی بڕۆین؟	How long should we go?
کامە؟	Which?	کامە پەرتووکی تۆیە؟	Which one is your book?

The Possesive Suffixes with the Pronoun هەموو

هەموو = all	Example	Meaning
هەموومان *all of us*	هەموومان دەڕۆن بۆ هەولێر.	We all are going to Hewlêr (Erbil)
هەموتان *all of you*	ئەم ماڵەکە بۆ هەموتانە.	This house is for all of you.
هەمویان *all of them*	هەمویان دەڕۆن بۆ ماڵەوە.	All of them are going home.
هەمووی *all of it*	هەمووی دەدەم بۆ تۆ.	I give all of it to you.

The Demonstrative Pronouns

The Pronouns	near	far
as a <u>noun</u>	مەئە (this) ئەمە منم. (This is me.) ئەمانە (these) ئەمانە ئێمەین. (These are us.)	ئەوە (that) ئەوە منم. (That is me.) وانەئە (those) ئەوانە ئێمەین. (Those are us.)
as an <u>adjective</u> ژن : woman دەرگا : door	ئەم ... (ی) ە ئەم ژنە (this woman) ئەم دەرگایە (this door) ئەم ...انە ئەم ژنانە (these women) ئەم دەرگانە (these doors)	ئەو ... (ی) ە ئەو ژنە (that woman) ئەو دەرگایە (that door) ئەو ...انە ئەو ژنانە (those women) ئەو دەرگانە (those doors)

THE PRONOUNS

The Reflexive Pronoun

خۆ + Personal ending	my/your/him/her/it(**self**) our/your/them(**selves**)

 خۆ applies to personal pronouns. It replaces the pronouns in a sentence, if it refers to the subject of the sentence:

من خۆم دەبینم.	I see **myself**.
تۆ خۆت دەبینیت.	You see **yourself**.
ئەو خۆی دەبینێت.	He/She/It sees **him/her/itself**.
ئێمە خۆمان دەبینین.	We see **ourselves**.
ئێوە خۆتان دەبینن.	You see **yourselves**.
ئەوان خۆیان دەبینن.	They see **themselves**.

 خۆ also replaces the possessive pronouns.

تۆ لە ماڵی منی.	You are in **my** house.

If the owner is identical to the subject:

من لە ماڵی خۆمم.	I am in **my** house.
تۆ لە ماڵی خۆتی.	You are in **your** house.
ئێمە لە ماڵی خۆمانین.	We are in **our** house.

 Alternative translation: ماڵ/ خانوو = *house*
من لە ماڵی خۆمم. = من لە خانووی خۆمدام.

The Reciprocal Pronoun

یەک / یەکتر	each other
ئێمە یەک دەبینین.	We see *each other*.
ئێمە یەکتر دەبینین.	We see *each other*.

Diminutive suffixes

Diminutivsuffixe	Meaning
ـۆکە	بزن (goat) → بزنۆکە (little goat)
ـۆچکە	شار (city) → شارۆچکە (small city)
ـۆلە	بەرخ (lamb) → بەرخۆلە (little lamb)
ـچە	باخ (field) → باخچە (garden)
ـژگە	کوڕ (boy) → کوڕژگە (little boy)
ـیلکە	چاو (eye) → چاویلکە (glasses)

💡 Some words which have the suffixes of diminution receive a new meaning.

Declension of nouns

Absolute state: This refers to a noun without an ending, which is also called the lexical form: ئاو (water), مامۆستا (teacher), خانوو (house)

Indefinite	Singular	Plural
Nouns ending with a vowel Endung مامۆستا (teacher) خانوو (house) دەرگا (door)	ـیەک مامۆستایەک (a teacher) خانوویەک (a house) دەرگایەک (a door)	ـ یان مامۆستایان (teacher) no plural no plural
Nouns ending with a consonant Endung ڕۆژ (day) ژن (woman)	ـێک ڕۆژێک (a day) ژنێک (a woman)	ـ ان ڕۆژان (days) ژنان (women)

💡 Most of **non-living things** (objects) have no plural version.

Declension of nouns

Definite	Singular	Plural
Nouns ending with a vowel Endung خانوو (house) دەرگا (door)	‍ـكە خانووكە (the house) دەرگاكەدە (the door)	‍ـكان خانووەكان (the houses) دەرگاكان (the doors)
Nouns ending with a consonant Endung ڕۆژ (day) ژن (woman)	‍ـەكە ڕۆژەكە (the day) ژنەكە (the woman)	‍ـەكان ڕۆژەكان (the days) ژنەكان (the women)

More Examples

Nouns can be described generally or specifically. In Sorani, this difference is established through endings. In daily use, however, the second variant dominates – even when speaking generally.

مامۆستایان باشن.	1. Teachers are good.
مامۆستاكان باشن.	2. The teachers are good.
مندااڵن زیرەكن.	1. Children are clever.
منداڵەكان زیرەكن.	2. The children are clever.
خانووەكان باشن.	The houses are good.
دەرگاكان جوانن.	The doors are beautiful.
هەندێ ڕۆژان/ هەندێ ژنان	some days / some women

Declension of nouns

Ezafe	Ending with a consonant	Ending with a vowel
absolute there is no plural form	– ە or ی – کچە جوان or کچی جوان (beautifil girl)	– ی ورگە رگایەدە (big door)
Definite		
Singular	– ە ... ەکە کچە جوانەکە (the beautiful girl)	**کە** – ... no suffix دەرگا گەورەکە (the big door)
Plural	– ە ... ەکان کچە جوانەکان (the beautiful girls)	**کان** – ... no suffix دەرگا گەورەکان (the big doors)
Indefinite		
Singular	– یەکی – or – ە ... ێک or کچێکی جوان کچە جوانێک (a beautiful girl)	– یەکی دەرگایەکی گەورە (eine größe Tür)
Plural very rare	– انی کچانی جوان (beautiful girls)	– نی ورگە رگانیەدە (big doors)

 In everyday life کچە جوانەکان or کچی جوان are used instead کچانی جوان.

e.g.: some beautiful girls = هەندێ کچی جوان
some big doors = هەندێ دەرگای گەورە

Vocative	Definite	
feminine **masculine** **Plural**	ێ - (Girl!) کچێ! (Aunt!) پووریێ! ە - (Boy!) کورە! (Uncle!) مامە! ینە- (Girls!) کچینە! (Boys!) کورینە!	Vocative case is not used for proper names.

The verb "to be" in present tense

The personal endings are used to express **"to be"**. The endings are added after an adjective or noun as well as in a verb conjugation.

Personal ending	Conjugation	Negation
1st Person Sg. - م	من جوانم. I am beautiful.	من جوان نیم. I am not beautiful.
2nd Person Sg. - یت	تۆ جوانیت. You are beautiful.	تۆ جوان نیت. You are not beautiful.
3rd Person Sg. - ە	ئەو جوانە. He/She/It is beautiful.	ئەو جوان نییە. He/She/It isn't beautiful.
1st Person Pl. - ین	ئێمە جوانین. We are beautiful.	ئێمە جوان نیین. We are not beautiful.
2nd Person Pl. - ن	ئێوە جوانن. You are beautiful.	ئێوە جوان نین. You are not beautiful.
3rd Person Pl. - ن	ئەوان جوانن. They are beautiful.	ئەوان جوان نین. They are not beautiful.

The verb "to be" in past tense

Personal ending	Conjugation	Negation
1st Person Sg. - م	من جوان بووم. I was beautiful.	من جوان نەبووم. I wasn't beautiful.
2nd Person Sg. - یت	تۆ جوان بوویت. You were beautiful.	تۆ جوان نەبوویت. You weren't beautiful.
3rd Person Sg. **No ending**	ئەو جوان بوو. He/She/It was beautiful	ئەو جوان نەبوو. He/She/It wasn't beautiful
1st Person Pl. - ین	ئێمە جوان بووین. We were beautiful.	ئێمە جوان نەبووین. We weren't beautiful.
2nd Person Pl. - ن	ئێوە جوان بوون. You were beautiful.	ئێوە جوان نەبوون. You weren't beautiful.
3rd Person Pl. - ن	ئەوان جوان بوون. They were beautiful.	ئەوان جوان نەبوون. They weren't beautiful.

THE PRESENT TENSE
Present Progressive & Simple Present Tense
Both tenses are the same in Sorani.

Formation of regular verbs:		
Preverb (-دە) + Present stem + Personal ending		
Preverb (-نا) + Present stem + Personal ending		
Example: چوون - *to go*		Verb stem: -چ-
Conjugation	من دەچم.	I go/I'm going.
	تۆ دەچیت.	You go/are going.
	ئەو دەچێت.	He/She/It goes/is going.
	ئێمە دەچین.	We go/are coming.
	ئێوە دەچن.	You go/are going. (*polite*)
	ئەوان دەچن.	They go /are going.
Negation (نا instead of دە) نا - not	من ناچم.	I don't go.
	تۆ ناچیت.	You don't go.
	ئەو ناچێت.	He/She/It doesn't go.
	ئێمە ناچین.	We don't go.
	ئێوە ناچن.	You don't go.
	ئەوان ناچن.	They don't go.
Interrogative Can be formed with or without ئایا	من دەچم؟	Do I go?
	تۆ دەچیت؟	Do you go?
	ئەو دەچێت؟	Does he/she/it go?
	ئێمە دەچین؟	Do we go?
	ئێوە دەچن؟	Do you go?
	ئەوان دەچن؟	Do they go?
Interrogative + Negation	من ناچم؟	Do I not go?
	تۆ ناچیت؟	Do you not go?
	ئەو ناچێت؟	Does he/she/it not go?

THE PRESENT TENSE

Can be formed with or without نایا	ئێمە ناچین؟	Do we not go?
	ئێوە ناچن؟	Do you not go?
	ئەوان ناچن؟	Do they not go?

 In some regions, -د letter of the preverb -دە is mostly neglected. In this case the conjugation: من ئەچم = *I go*

 In some regions, the letter -ت of the third person singular is neglected as well: ئەو دەچێ = *He/She/It goes.*

Formation of separable compound verbs:		
<u>Prefix</u> + Preverb (-دە) + Present stem + Personal ending <u>Prefix</u> + Preverb (-نا) + Present stem + Personal ending		
Example: دا-نیشتن - *to sit (down)*		Verb stem: دا - نیش
Conjugation	من دادەنیشم.	I sit (down)/am sitting.
	تۆ دادەنیشیت.	You sit (down).
	ئەو دادەنیشێت.	He/She/It sits (down).
	ئێمە دادەنیشین.	We sit (down).
	ئێوە دادەنیشن.	You sit (down).
	ئەوان دادەنیشن.	They sit (down).
Negation (نا instead of دە) نا - not	من دانانیشم.	I don't sit (down).
	تۆ دانانیشیت.	You don't sit (down).
	ئەو دانانیشێت.	He/She/It doesn't sit (down).
	ئێمە دانانیشین.	We don't sit (down).
	ئێوە دانانیشن.	You don't sit (down).
	ئەوان دانانیشن.	They don't sit (down).
Interrogative Can be formed with or without ئایا	من دادەنیشم؟	Do I sit (down)?
	تۆ دادەنیشیت؟	Do you sit (down)?
	ئەو دادەنیشێت؟	Does he/she sit (down)?

THE PRESENT TENSE

	ئێمە دادەنیشین؟	Do we sit (down)?
	ئێوە دادەنیشن؟	Do you sit (down)?
	ئەوان دادەنیشن؟	Do they sit (down)?
Interrogative + Negation Can be formed with or without ئایا	من دانانیشم؟	Do I not sit (down)?
	تۆ دانانیشیت؟	Do you not sit (down)?
	ئەو دانانیشێت؟	Does he/she not sit (down)?
	ئێمە دانانیشین؟	Do we not sit (down)?
	ئێوە دانانیشن؟	Do you not sit (down)?
	ئەوان دانانیشن؟	Do they not sit (down)?

In some regions, the letter ت‍ of the third person singular is neglected: ئەو دادەنیشێ = *He/She sits/is sitting*

Formation of separable compound verbs with the suffix ‍ەوە-:		
Preverb (د‍ە-) + Present stem + Personal ending + ‍ەوە-		
Preverb (نا-) + Present stem + Personal ending + ‍ەوە-		
Example: گەڕانەوە - *to return*		Verb stem: گەڕێ-ەوە
Conjugation	من دەگەڕێمەوە.	I return/I am returning
	تۆ دەگەڕێیتەوە.	You return
	ئەو دەگەڕێیەوە.	He/She/It returns
	ئێمە دەگەڕێینەوە.	We return
	ئێوە دەگەڕێنەوە.	You return
	ئەوان دەگەڕێنەوە.	They return
Negation (نا instead of دە) نا - *not*	ناگەڕێمەوە.	I don't return
	ناگەڕێیتەوە.	You don't return
	ناگەڕێیەوە.	He/She/It doesn't return
	ناگەڕێینەوە.	We don't return
	ناگەڕێنەوە.	You don't return
	ناگەڕێنەوە.	They don't return

THE PRESENT TENSE

Interrogative Can be formed with or without ئایا	من دەگەڕێمەوە؟	Do I return?
	تۆ دەگەڕێیتەوە؟	Do you return?
	ئەو دەگەڕێیەوە؟	Does he/she/it return?
	ئێمە دەگەڕێینەوە؟	Do we return?
	ئێوە دەگەڕێنەوە؟	Do you return?
	ئەوان دەگەڕێنەوە؟	Do they return?
Interrogative + Negation Can be formed with or without ئایا	ناگەڕێمەوە؟	Do I not return?
	ناگەڕێیتەوە؟	Do you not return?
	ناگەڕێیەوە؟	Does he/she/it not return?
	ناگەڕێینەوە؟	Do we not return?
	ناگەڕێنەوە؟	Do you not return?
	ناگەڕێنەوە؟	Do they not return?

Formation of irregular verbs:		
Preverb (-دە) + Present stem + Personal ending		
Preverb (-نا) + Present stem + Personal ending		
Example: وتن - *to say*		Verb stem: -ڵێ
Conjugation	من دەڵێم.	I say...
	تۆ دەڵێیت.	You say...
	ئەو دەڵێت.	He/She/It says...
	ئێمە دەڵێین.	We say...
	ئێوە دەڵێن.	You say...
	ئەوان دەڵێن.	They say...
Negation (نا instead of دە) نا - *not*	من ناڵێم.	I don't say...
	تۆ ناڵێیت.	You don't say...
	ئەو ناڵێت.	He/She/It doesn't say...
	ئێمە ناڵێین.	We don't say...
	ئێوە ناڵێن.	You don't say...
	ئەوان ناڵێن.	They don't say...
Interrogative	من دەڵێم؟	Do I say...?

THE PRESENT TENSE

Can be formed with or without ئایا	تۆ دەڵێیت؟	Do you say...?
	ئەو دەڵێت؟	Does he/she/it say...?
	ئێمە دەڵێین؟	Do we say...?
	ئێوە دەڵێن؟	Do you say...?
	ئەوان دەڵێن؟	Do they say...?
Interrogative + Negation Can be formed with or without ئایا	من ناڵێم؟	Do I not say...?
	تۆ ناڵێیت؟	Do you say...?
	ئەو ناڵێت؟	Does he/she/it not say...?
	ئێمە ناڵێین؟	Do we not say...?
	ئێوە ناڵێن؟	Do you not say...?
	ئەوان ناڵێن؟	Do they not say...?

Formation of regular verbs with an object:		
Preverb (دە-) + Past stem + Personal ending		
Preverb (نا-) + Past stem + Personal ending		
Example: بینین - *to see*		Verb stem: -بین-
Conjugation **with object**	من ئەو دەبینم.	I see him/her/it.
	تۆ ئەو دەبینیت.	You see him/her/it.
	ئەو ئەو دەبینێت.	He/She/It sees him/her/it
	ئێمە ئەو دەبینین.	We see him/her/it.
	ئێوە ئەو دەبینن.	You see him/her/it.
	ئەوان ئەو دەبینن.	They see him/her/it.
Negation (نا instead of دە)	من ئەو نابینم.	I don't see him/her/it.
	تۆ ئەو نابینیت.	You don't see him/her/it.
	ئەو ئەو نابینێت.	He/She/It don't see him/her/it.
	ئێمە ئەو نابینین.	We don't see him/her/it.
	ئێوە ئەو نابینن.	You don't see him/her/it.
	ئەوان ئەو نابینن.	They don't see him/her/it.

Pronominal Objects in present tense

Object pronouns of the present tense or imperative are normally attached to some part of the verbal construction. If there is a compound verb, the pronouns attach to the first part (a *noun*, an *adjective,* or a *prefix*) of the verb. If the verb is not compound, the pronouns attach after the preverb (مه‌ ،‌ ب- ،‌ نا- ،‌ ده-). Pronominal object endings are used only with transitive verbs.

after a consonant		Example
م-	me	په‌نهانم ده‌که‌یت (You hide **me**)
		په‌نهانم ناکه‌یت (You don't hide **me**)
ت-	you	په‌نهانت ده‌که‌م (I hide **you**)
		په‌نهانت ناکه‌م (I don't hide **you**)
ی-	him/her/it	په‌نهانی ده‌که‌م (I hide **him/her/it**)
		په‌نهانی ناکه‌م (I don't hide **him/her/it**)
مان-	us	په‌نهانمان ده‌که‌م (I hide **us**)
		په‌نهانمان ناکه‌م (I don't hide **us**)
تان-	you	په‌نهانتان ده‌که‌م (I hide **you**)
		په‌نهانتان ناکه‌م (I don't hide **you**)
تان-	them	په‌نهانیان ده‌که‌م (I hide **them**)
		په‌نهانیان ناکه‌م (I don't hide **them**)
after a vowel		
م-	me	ده‌مبینێت (You see **me**)
		نامبینێت (You don't see **me**)
ت-	you	ده‌تبینم (I see **you**)
		ناتبینم (I don't see **you**)
ی-	him/her/it	ده‌یبینم (I see **him/her/it**)
		نایبینم (I don't see **him/her/it**)
مان-	us	ده‌مانبینم (I see **us**)
		نامانبینم (I don't see **us**)
تان-	you	ده‌تانبینم (I see **you**)
		ناتانبینم (I don't see **you**)

	them	دەیانبینم (I see them)
ـتان		نایانبینم (I don't see them)

 خۆم پەنهان دەکەم = I hide *myself*

خۆم دەبینم = I see *myself*

The Imperative

Formation	Verb	Imperative
ب + Verb stem + ە (2nd person, Singular) مە + Verb stem + ە (If the verb stem ends on a vowel, that vowel is used instead of ە -)	کردن (to do) Verb stem: ـکە-	بکە! (Do!) مەکە! (Don't do!)
	نووسین (to write) Verb stem: ـنووس-	بنووسە! (Write!) مەنووسە! (Don't write!)
	رۆیشتن (to go) Verb stem: ـرۆ-	برۆ! (Go!) مەرۆ ! (Don't go!)
ب + Verb stem + ن (2nd person, Plural) مە + Verb stem + ن	کردن Verb stem: ـکە-	بکەن! (Do!) مەکەن! (Don't do!)
	نووسین Verb stem: ـنووس-	بنووسن! (Write!) مەنووسن! (Don't write!)
	رۆیشتن Verb stem: ـرۆ-	برۆن! (Go!) مەرۆن! (Don't go!)
with *Pronominal objects*	بینووسە! (Write *it*!)	مەینووسە! (Don't write it!)
	بیاننووسە! (Write *them*!)	مەیاننووسە! (Don't write them!)

نییه / هەیە

هەیە: to have There is/are	نییه: not to have there is/are not
یەهە (singular) من دەفتەرێکم هەیە (I have a notebook.) دەفتەرێک لەوێ هەیە. (There is a notebook over there.)	نییه (singular) من دەفتەرێکم نییه. (I don't have a notebook.) هیچ دەفتەرێک لەوێ نییه. (There isn't a notebook over there.)
یەهە (Pl.) من پێنووسم هەیە (I have pens.) لەوێ پێنووس هەیە. (There are pens over there.)	نییه (Pl.) من پێنووسم نییه. (I don't have pens.) لەوێ پێنووس نییه. (There aren't pens over there.)

Alternative: من پێنووسم پێیە = من پێنووسم هەیە
  من پێنووسم پێ نییه = من پێنووسم نییه

The Modal Verbs

Modal verb	Conjugation	Negation
ویستن (to want) Verb stem -وێته-	دە+Personal ending+وێت	نا + Personal ending + وێت
	من دەمەوێت (I want)	من نامەوێت (I don't want)
	تۆ دەتەوێت (You want)	تۆ ناتەوێت (You don't want)
	ئەو دەیەوێت (He/She/It wants)	ئەو نایەوێت (He/She/It doesn't want)
	ئێمە دەمانەوێت (We want)	ئێمە نامانەوێت (We don't want)
	دەتانەوێت (You want)	ئێوە ناتانەوێت (You don't want)

The Modal Verbs

	ئەوان دەیانەوێت (They want)	ئەوانە ناویان ئەوێت (They don't want)

💡 In some regions of Kurdistan, short forms are used:
(I want) ئەمەوێ ← ئەمەوێت ← دەمەوێت

Modal verb	Conjugation	Negation
توانین (can) Verb stem - توان-	دە + توان + P. ending	نا + توان + Personal ending
	من دەتوانم (I can)	من ناتوانم (I can't)
	تۆ دەتوانیت (You can)	تۆ ناتوانیت (You can't)
	ئەو دەتوانی (He/She/It can)	ئەو ناتوانیت (He/She/It can't)
	ئێمە دەتوانین (We can)	ئێمە ناتوانین (We can't)
	ئێوە دەتوانن (You can)	ئێوە ناتوانن (You can't)
	ئەوان دەتوانن (They can)	ئەوان ناتوانن (They can't)

دەبێتده or دەبێ (must, have to, should) دەبێ remains unchanged	من دەبێ (I must/should/have to)	نە + Verb stem of the main verb + Personal ending
	تۆ دەبێ (You must)	
	ئەو دەبێ (He/She/It must)	
	ئێمە دەبێ (We must)	
	ئێوە دەبێ (You must)	

| | ئەوان دەبێ (They must) | |

 When *conjugating/negating* دەبێ a main verb is obligatory. This means that you can not only say: „I must (not)"

e.g.: دەبێ بخۆم/نەخۆم = I must (not) eat

The Subjunctive with Modal Verbs

Conjugation:	دەبێ & ب + Present stem + Personal ending
Negation:	دەبێ & نە + Present stem + Personal ending

Conjugation	Negation
دەبێ من بخۆم.	دەبێ من نەخۆم.
(I must/have to eat.)	(I must **not** eat.)
دەبێ تۆ بخۆیت.	دەبێ تۆ نەخۆیت.
(You must/have to eat.)	(You must **not** to eat.)
دەبێ ئەو بخوات.	دەبێ ئەو نەخوات.
(He/She/It must/have to eat.)	(He/She/It must **not** eat.)
دەبێ ئێمە بخۆین.	دەبێ ئێمە نەخۆین.
(We must/have to eat.)	(We must **not** eat.)
دەبێ ئێوە بخۆن.	دەبێ ئێوە نەخۆن.
(You must/have to eat.)	(You must **not** eat.)
دەبێ ئەوان بخۆن.	دەبێ ئەوان نەخۆن.
(They must/have to eat.)	(They must **not** to eat.)

Conjugation of Modal verbs (توانین or ویستن) &
ب + Present stem + Personal ending
Negation of Modal verbs (توانین or ویستن) &
ب + Present stem + Personal ending

The Subjunctive with Modal Verbs

Conjugation	Negation
من دەتوانم بخۆم. (I can eat.)	من ناتوانم بخۆم. (I can't eat.)
من دەمەوێت بخۆم. (I want to eat.)	من نامەوێت بخۆم. (I don't want to eat.)
تۆ دەتوانیت بخۆیت. (You can eat.)	تۆ ناتوانیت بخۆیت. (You can't eat.)
تۆ دەتەوێت بخۆیت. (You want to eat.)	تۆ ناتەوێت بخۆیت. (You don't want to eat.)
ئەو دەتوانێت بخوات. (He/She/It can eat.)	ئەو ناتوانێت بخوات. (He/She/It can't eat.)
ئەو دەیەوێت بخوات. (He/She/It wants to eat.)	ئەو نایەوێت بخوات. (He/She/It doesn't want to eat.)
ئێمە دەتوانین بخۆین. (We can eat.)	ئێمە ناتوانین بخۆین. (We can't eat.)
ئێمە دەمانەوێت بخۆین. (We want to eat.)	ئێمە نامانەوێت بخۆین. (We don't want to eat.)
ئێوە دەتوانن بخۆن. (You can eat.)	ئێوە ناتوانن بخۆن. (You can't eat.)
ئێوە دەتانەوێت بخۆن. (You want to eat.)	ئێوە ناتانەوێت بخۆن. (You don't want to eat.)
ئەوان دەتوانن بخۆن. (They can eat.)	ئەوان ناتوانن بخۆن. (They can't eat.)
ئەوان دەیانەوێت بخۆن. (They want to eat.)	ئەوان نایانەوێت بخۆن. (They don't want to eat.)

You can use the synonym خواستن instead of ویستن.

e.g.: من دەخوازم ← من دەمەوێت (I want)

من دەخوازم بخۆم ← من دەمەوێت بخۆم (I want to eat)

من ناخوازم بخۆم ← من نامەوێت بخۆم (I don't want to eat)

THE PAST TENSES

Personal endings for the intransitive verbs	Personal endings for the transitive verbs	Personen
ـم	ـم	1st Person Sg.
ـیت	ـت	2nd Person Sg.
No ending	ـی	3rd Person Sg.
ـین	ـمان	1st Person Pl.
ـن	ـتان	2nd Person Pl.
ـن	ـیان	3rd Person Pl.

The Simple Past Tense

This tense expresses a one-off act in the past.

Formation of intransitive verbs:
Past stem + Personal ending
Preverb (ـنە) + Past stem + Personal ending

Example: هاتن - *to come*		Verb stem: -هات-
Conjugation	من هاتم.	I came.
	تۆ هاتیت.	You came.
	ئەو هات.	He/She/It came.
	ئێمە هاتین.	We came.
	ئێوە هاتن.	You came.
	ئەوان هاتن.	They came.
Negation نە - *not*	من نەهاتم.	I didn't come.
	تۆ نەهاتیت.	You didn't come.
	ئەو نەهات.	He/She/It didn't come.
	ئێمە نەهاتین.	We didn't come.
	ئێوە نەهاتن.	You didn't come.
	ئەوان نەهاتن.	They didn't come.
	من هاتم؟	Did I come?

THE PAST TENSES

Interrogative Can be formed with or without ئایا	تۆ هاتیت؟	Did you come?
	ئەو هات؟	Did he/she/it come?
	ئێمە هاتین؟	Did we come?
	ئێوە هاتن؟	Did you come?
	ئەوان هاتن؟	Did they come?
Interrogative + Negation Can be formed with or without ئایا	من نەهاتم؟	Did I not come?
	تۆ نەهاتیت؟	Did you not come?
	ئەو نەهات؟	Did he/she/it not come?
	ئێمە نەهاتین؟	Did we not come?
	ئێوە نەهاتن؟	Did you not come?
	ئەوان نەهاتن؟	Did they not come?

Formation of intransitive compound verbs:

Prefix + Past stem + Personal ending

Prefix + Preverb (-نە) + Past stem + Personal ending

Example: هەڵسان - *to stand up*		Verb stem: هەڵ_سا
Conjugation	من هەڵسام.	I stood up.
	تۆ هەڵسایت.	You stood up.
	ئەو هەڵسا.	He/She/It stood up.
	ئێمە هەڵساین.	We stood up.
	ئێوە هەڵسان.	You stood up.
	ئەوان هەڵسان.	They stood up.
Negation نە - not	من هەڵنەسام.	I didn't stand up.
	تۆ هەڵنەسایت.	You didn't stand up.
	ئەو هەڵنەسا.	He/She/It didn't stand up.
	ئێمە هەڵنەساین.	We didn't stand up.
	ئێوە هەڵنەسان.	You didn't stand up.

THE PAST TENSES

	ئەوان هەڵنەسان.	They didn't stand up.
Interrogative Can be formed with or without ئایا	من هەڵسام؟	Did I stand up?
	تۆ هەڵسایت؟	Did you stand up?
	ئەو هەڵسا؟	Did he/she/it stand up?
	ئێمە هەڵساین؟	Did we stand up?
	ئێوە هەڵسان؟	Did you stand up?
	ئەوان هەڵسان؟	Did they stand up?
Interrogative + Negation Can be formed with or without ئایا	من هەڵنەسام؟	Did I not stand up?
	تۆ هەڵنەسایت؟	Did you stand up?
	ئەو هەڵنەسا؟	Did he/she/it not stand up?
	ئێمە هەڵنەساین؟	Did we not stand up?
	ئێوە هەڵنەسان؟	Did you not stand up?
	ئەوان هەڵنەسان؟	Did they not stand up?

If the verb is *intransitive,* it does not get separated in simple past, pluperfect & present perfect tenses *(except for negations)*.

Formation of separable compound verbs with the suffix -ەوە:		
Past stem + Personal ending + -ەوە		
Preverb (-نە) + Past stem + Personal ending + -ەوە		
Example: گەڕانەوە - *to return*		Verb stem: گەڕا-ەوە
Conjugation	من گەڕامەوە.	I returned
	تۆ گەڕایتەوە.	You returned
	ئەو گەڕایەوە.	He/She/It returned
	ئێمە گەڕاینەوە.	We returned
	ئێوە گەڕانەوە.	You returned
	ئەوان گەڕانەوە.	They returned
Negation	من نەگەڕامەوە.	I did not return
	تۆ نەگەڕایتەوە.	You did not return
	ئەو نەگەڕایەوە.	He/She/It not return

THE PAST TENSES

نە - not	ئێمە نەگەڕاینەوە.	We did not return
	ئێوە نەگەڕانەوە.	You did not return
	ئەوان نەگەڕانەوە.	They did not return
Interrogative Can be formed with or without ئایا	ئایا من گەڕامەوە؟	Did I return?
	ئایا تۆ گەڕایتەوە؟	Did you return?
	ئایا ئەو گەڕایەوە؟	Did he/she/it return?
	ئایا ئێمە گەڕاینەوە؟	Did we return?
	ئایا ئێوە گەڕانەوە؟	Did you return?
	ئایا ئەوان گەڕانەوە؟	Did they return?
Interrogative + Negation Can be formed with or without ئایا	من نەگەڕامەوە؟	Did I not return?
	تۆ نەگەڕایتەوە؟	Did you not return?
	ئەو نەگەڕایەوە؟	Did he/she/it not return?
	ئێمە نەگەڕاینەوە؟	Did we not return?
	ئێوە نەگەڕانەوە؟	Did you not return?
	ئەوان نەگەڕانەوە؟	Did they not return?

Formation of transitive verbs:

Past stem + Personal ending

Preverb (-نە) + Personal ending + Past stem

Example: بینین - *to see*		Verb stem: -بینی
Conjugation **without object**	من بینیم.	I saw.
	تۆ بینیت.	You saw.
	ئەو بینی.	He/She/It saw.
	ئێمە بینیمان.	We saw.
	ئێوە بینیتان.	You saw.
	ئەوان بینییان.	They saw.
Negation	من نەمبینی.	I didn't see
	تۆ نەتبینی.	You didn't see
	ئەو نەیبینی.	He/She/It didn't see

THE PAST TENSES

نه - not	ئێمه نه‌مانبینی.	We didn't see
	ئێوه نه‌تانبینی.	You didn't see
	ئه‌وان نه‌یانبینی.	They didn't see
Interrogative Can be formed with or without ئایا	من بینیم؟	Did I see?
	تۆ بینیت؟	Did you see?
	ئه‌و بینی؟	Did he/she/it see?
	ئێمه بینیمان؟	Did we see?
	ئێوه بینیتان؟	Did you see?
	ئه‌وان بینییان؟	Did they see?
Interrogative + Negation Can be formed with or without ئایا	من نه‌مبینی؟	Did I not see?
	تۆ نه‌تبینی؟	Did you not see?
	ئه‌و نه‌یبینی؟	Did he/she not see?
	ئێمه نه‌مانبینی؟	Did we not see?
	ئێوه نه‌تانبینی؟	Did you not see?
	ئه‌وان نه‌یانبینی؟	Did they not see?

 A personal pronoun is not obligatory.

من بینیم = بینیم = I saw

من نه‌مبینی = نه‌مبینی = I didn't see

Formation of transitive verbs „with an object"
Object + Personal ending & Past stem

Object + Personal ending & Preverb (-نه) + Past stem

Example: بینین - *to see*		Verb stem: -بینی-
Conjugation **with object**	من ئه‌وم بینی.	I saw him/her/it.
	تۆ ئه‌وت بینی.	You saw him/her/it.
	ئه‌و ئه‌وی بینی.	He/She/It saw him/her/it.
	ئێمه ئه‌ومان بینی.	We saw him/her/it.
	ئێوه ئه‌وتان بینی.	You saw him/her/it.
	ئه‌وان ئه‌ویان بینی.	They saw him/her/it.
Negation	من ئه‌وم نه‌بینی.	I didn't see him/her/it.
	تۆ ئه‌وت نه‌بینی.	You didn't see him/her/it.

THE PAST TENSES

نه - not	ئەو ئەوی نەبینی.	He/She/It didn't see him/her/it.
	ئێمە ئەومان نەبینی.	We didn't see him/her/it.
	ئێوە ئەوتان نەبینی.	You didn't see him/her/it.
	ئەوان ئەویان نەبینی.	They didn't see him/her/it.

More Examples

Conjugation with object	من تۆم بینی.	I saw you.
	من ئەوانم بینی.	I saw them.
	تۆ منت بینی.	You saw me.
	ئەو ئێمەی بینی.	He/She/It saw us.
	ئێمە ئەوانمان بینی.	We saw them.
	ئێوە منتان بینی.	You saw us.
	ئەوان ئێوەیان بینی.	They saw you.

When a transitive verb is used in the past with an object, the personal ending is not attached to the verb but to the object.

e.g.: من بینیم = I saw - من تۆم بینی = I saw you

Negation	من تۆم نەبینی.	I didn't see you.
	تۆ منت نەبینی.	You didn't see me.
نه - not	ئەو ئێمەی نەبینی.	He/She/It didn't see us.
	ئەو ئەوی نەبینی.	She didn't see him/her/it.
	ئێمە ئەوانمان نەبینی.	We didn't see them.
	ئێوە منتان نەبینی.	You didn't see me.
	ئەوان ئێوەیان نەبینی.	They didn't see you.

THE PAST TENSES

Comparison of Present and Past tenses

Present Tense	Past Tense
من تۆ دەبینم I see you.	من تۆم بینی I saw you.
تۆ من دەبینیت You see me.	تۆ منت بینی You saw me
من ئەو دەبینم I see him/her/it.	من ئەوم بینی I saw him/her/it.
ئەو من دەبینێت He/She sees me.	ئەو منی بینی He/She saw me.
من ئێمە دەبینم I see us.	من ئێمەم بینی I saw us.
ئێمە تۆ دەبینین We see you.	ئێمە تۆمان بینی We saw you.
من ئێوە دەبینم I see you. (plural)	من ئێوەم بینی I saw you. (plural)
ئێوە من دەبینن You see me.	ئێوە منتان بینی You saw me.
من ئەوان دەبینم Ich sehe sie. (Plural)	من ئەوانم بینی Ich sah sie. (Plural)
ئەوان من دەبینن They see me.	ئەوان منیان بینی They saw me.
بێریڤان من دەبینێت Bêrîvan sees me.	بێریڤان منی بینی Bêrîvan saw me. (a female name)
من بێریڤان دەبینم I see Bêrîvan.	من بێریڤانم بینی I saw Bêrîvan.

 When a transitive verb is used in the past with an object, the personal ending is not attached to the verb but to the object.

The Past Progressive Tense

The Sorani past progressive tense expresses events in the past, which lasted for a long period of time or reoccurred regularly.

Formation of intransitive verbs:		
Preverb (ده-) + Past stem + Personal ending		
Preverb (دەنە-) + Past stem + Personal ending		
Example: هاتن - *to come*		Verb stem: -هات-
Conjugation	من دەهاتم.	I was coming. (*repeatedly* or *last for a long period of time*)
	تۆ دەهاتیت.	You were coming.
	ئەو دەهات.	He/She/It was coming.
	ئێمە دەهاتین.	We were coming.
	ئێوە دەهاتن.	You were coming.
	ئەوان دەهاتن.	They were coming.
Negation نە - *not*	من نەدەهاتم.	I was not coming.
	تۆ نەدەهاتیت.	You weren't coming.
	ئەو نەدەهات.	He/She/It wasn't coming.
	ئێمە نەدەهاتین.	We weren't coming.
	ئێوە نەدەهاتن.	You weren't coming.
	ئەوان نەدەهاتن.	They weren't coming.
Interrogative Can be formed with or without ئایا	من دەهاتم؟	Was I coming?
	تۆ دەهاتیت؟	We you coming?
	ئەو دەهات؟	Was he/she/it coming?
	ئێمە دەهاتین؟	Were we coming?
	ئێوە دەهاتن؟	Were you coming?
	ئەوان دەهاتن؟	Were they coming?
Interrogative + Negation	من نەدەهاتم؟	Was I not coming?
	تۆ نەدەهاتیت؟	We you not coming?
	ئەو نەدەهات؟	Was he/she/it not coming?

THE PAST TENSES

Can be formed with or without ئایا	ئێمە نەدەهاتین؟	Were we not coming?
	ئێوە نەدەهاتن؟	Were you not coming?
	ئەوان نەدەهاتن؟	Were they not coming?

Formation of transitive verbs:

Preverb (دە-) + Personal ending + Past stem

Preverb (نە-) + Personal ending + Preverb (دە-) + Past stem

Example: بینین - *to see*		Verb stem: -بینی-
Conjugation **without object**	من دەمبینی.	I was seeing. (repeatedly or last for a long period of time)
	تۆ دەتبینی.	You were seeing.
	ئەو دەیبینی.	He/She/It was seeing.
	ئێمە دەمانبینی.	We were seeing.
	ئێوە دەتانبینی.	You were seeing.
	ئەوان دەیانبینی.	They were seeing.
Negation نە – *not* No difference **with** or **without** pronouns	نەمدەبینی.	I was **not** seeing.
	نەتدەبینی.	You weren't seeing.
	نەیدەبینی.	He/She wasn't seeing.
	نەماندەبینی.	We weren't seeing.
	نەتاندەبینی.	You weren't seeing.
	نەیاندەبینی.	They weren't seeing.
Interrogative Can be formed with or without ئایا	من دەمبینی؟	Was I seeing?
	تۆ دەتبینی؟	Were you seeing?
	ئەو دەیبینی؟	Was he/she/it seeing?
	ئێمە دەمانبینی؟	Were we seeing?
	ئێوە دەتانبینی؟	Were you seeing?
	ئەوان دەیانبینی؟	Were they seeing?
Interrogative + Negation	من نەمدەبینی؟	Was I not seeing?
	تۆ نەتدەبینی؟	Were you not seeing?
	ئەو نەیدەبینی؟	Was he/she not seeing?

THE PAST TENSES

Can be formed with or without ئایا	ئێمە نەماندەبینی؟	Were we not seeing?
	ئێوە نەتاندەبینی؟	Were you not seeing?
	ئەوان نەیاندەبینی؟	Were they not seeing?

Formation of transitive verbs „with an object"

Object + Personal ending & Preverb (د‍ە-) + Past stem
Object + Personal ending & Preverb (دە‍نە-) + Past stem

Example: بینین - *to see*		Verb stem: -بینی-
Conjugation **with object**	من ئەوم دەبینی.	I was seeing him/her/it.
	تۆ ئەوت دەبینی.	You were seeing him/her/it.
	ئەو ئەوی دەبینی.	He/She/It was seeing him/her/it.
	ئێمە ئەومان دەبینی.	We were seeing him/her/it.
	ئێوە ئەوتان دەبینی.	You were seeing him/her/it.
	ئەوان ئەویان دەبینی.	They were seeing him/her/it.
Negation نە – *not* No difference **with** or **without** pronouns	من ئەوم نەدەبینی.	I wasn't seeing him/her/it.
	تۆ ئەوت نەدەبینی.	You weren't seeing him/her/it.
	ئەو ئەوی نەدەببنی.	He/She/It wasn't seeing hIm/her/lt.
	ئێمە ئەومان نەدەبینی.	We weren't seeing him/her/it.
	ئێوە ئەوتان نەدەبینی.	You weren't seeing him.
	ئەوان ئەویان نەدەبینی.	They weren't seeing him/her/it.

THE PAST TENSES

More Examples in the Past Progressive Tense

Conjugation **with object**	.من تۆم دەبینی	I was seeing you.
	.تۆ منت دەبینی	You were seeing me.
	.ئەو ئێمەی دەبینی	He/She/It was seeing us.
	.ئەو ئەوی دەبینی	He/She was seeing him/her/it.
	.ئێمە ئەوانمان دەبینی	We were seeing them.
	.ئێوە منتان دەبینی	You were seeing me.
	.ئەوان ئێویان دەبینی	They were seeing you.
Negation **نە - not**	.تۆم نەدەبینی	I wasn't seeing you.
	.منت نەدەبینی	You weren't seeing me.
	.ئێمەی نەدەبینی	He/She wasn't seeing us.
	.ئەوی نەدەبینی	He/She/It wasn't seeing him/her/it.
	.ئەوانمان نەدەبینی	We weren't seeing them.
	.منتان نەدەبینی	You weren't seeing me.
	.ئێویان نەدەبینی	They weren't seeing you.

Formation of intransitive compound verbs:

Prefix + Preverb (دە-) + Past stem + Personal ending

Prefix + Preverb (دەنە-) + Past stem + Personal ending

Example: هەڵستان - *to stand up*		Verb stem: هەڵ-سا
Conjugation	.من هەڵدەسام	I was standing up. **(repeatedly or last for a long period of time)**
	.تۆ هەڵدەسایت	You were standing up.
	.ئەو هەڵدەسا	He/She/It was standing up.
	.ئێمە هەڵدەساین	We were standing up.
	.ئێوە هەڵدەسان	You were standing up.
	.ئەوان هەڵدەسان	They were standing up.

THE PAST TENSES 40

Negation نه - **not**	هەڵنەدەسام.	I was **not** standing up.
	تۆ هەڵنەدەسایت.	You weren't standing up.
	ئەو هەڵنەدەسا.	He/She/It wasn't standing up.
	ئێمە هەڵنەدەساین.	We weren't standing up.
	ئێوە هەڵنەدەسان.	You weren't standing up.
	ئەوان هەڵنەدەسان.	They weren't standing up.
Interrogative Can be formed with or without ئایا	من هەڵدەسام؟	Was I standing up?
	تۆ هەڵدەسایت؟	Were you standing up?
	ئەو هەڵدەسا؟	Was he/she standing up?
	ئێمە هەڵدەساین؟	Were we standing up?
	ئێوە هەڵدەسان؟	Were you standing up?
	ئەوان هەڵدەسان؟	Were they standing up?
Interrogative + Negation Can be formed with or without ئایا	هەڵنەدەسام؟	Was I not standing up?
	تۆ هەڵنەدەسایت؟	Were you not standing up?
	ئەو هەڵنەدەسا؟	Was he/she not standing up?
	ئێمە هەڵنەدەساین؟	Were we not standing up?
	ئێوە هەڵنەدەسان؟	Were you not standing up?
	ئەوان هەڵنەدەسان؟	Were they not standing up?

Formation of separable compound verbs with the suffix -ەوە :		
Preverb (-دە) + Past stem + Personal ending + -ەوە		
Preverb (-دەنە) + Past stem + Personal ending + -ەوە		
Example: گەڕانەوە - *to return*		Verb stem: گەڕا-دەوە
Conjugation	دەگەڕامەوە.	I was returning
	دەگەڕایتەوە.	You were returning
	دەگەڕایەوە.	He/She/It was returning
	دەگەڕاینەوە.	We were returning

THE PAST TENSES

	دەگەڕانەوە.	You were returning
	دەگەڕانەوە.	They were returning
Negation نە - not	نەدەگەڕامەوە.	I wasn't returning
	نەدەگەڕایتەوە.	You weren't returning
	نەدەگەڕایەوە.	He/She/It wasn't returning
	نەدەگەڕاینەوە.	We weren't returning
	نەدەگەڕانەوە.	You weren't returning
	نەدەگەڕانەوە.	They weren't returning
Interrogative Can be formed with or without ئایا	دەگەڕامەوە؟	Was I returning?
	دەگەڕایتەوە؟	Were you returning?
	دەگەڕایەوە؟	Was he/she/it returning?
	دەگەڕاینەوە؟	Were we returning?
	دەگەڕانەوە؟	Were you returning?
	دەگەڕانەوە؟	Were they returning?
Interrogative + Negation Can be formed with or without ئایا	نەدەگەڕامەوە؟	Was I not returning?
	نەدەگەڕایتەوە؟	Were you not returning?
	نەدەگەڕایەوە؟	Was he/she/it not returning?
	نەدەگەڕاینەوە؟	Were we not returning?
	نەدەگەڕانەوە؟	Were you not returning?
	نەدەگەڕانەوە؟	Were they not returning?

The Pluperfect Tense

When the completed action is even longer in the past than the simple past tense, the pluperfect tense is used.

Formation of intransitive verbs:		
Past stem + -بوو- + Personal ending		
Preverb (نه-) + Past stem + -بوو- + Personal ending		
Example: هاتن - *to come*		Verb stem: -هات-
Conjugation	من هاتبووم.	I had come.
	تۆ هاتبوویت.	You had come.
	ئەو هاتبوو.	He/She/It had come.
	ئێمە هاتبووین.	We had come.
	ئێوە هاتبوون.	You had come.
	ئەوان هاتبوون.	They had come.
Negation نه - not	من نەهاتبووم.	I had **not** come.
	تۆ نەهاتبوویت.	You had **not** come.
	ئەو نەهاتبوو.	He/She/It had **not** come.
	ئێمە نەهاتبووین.	We had **not** come.
	ئێوە نەهاتبوون.	You had **not** come.
	ئەوان نەهاتبوون.	They had **not** come.
Interrogative Can be formed with or without ئایا	من هاتبووم؟	Had I come?
	تۆ هاتبوویت؟	Had you come?
	ئەو هاتبوو؟	Had he/she/it come?
	ئێمە هاتبووین؟	Had we come?
	ئێوە هاتبوون؟	Had you come?
	ئەوان هاتبوون؟	Had they come?
	من نەهاتبووم؟	Had I not come?
	تۆ نەهاتبوویت؟	Had you not come?

THE PAST TENSES

Interrogative + Negation Can be formed with or without ئایا	ئەو نەھاتبوو؟	Had he/she/it not come?
	ئێمە نەھاتبووین؟	Had we not come?
	ئێوە نەھاتبوون؟	Had you not come?
	ئەوان نەھاتبوون؟	Had they not come?

Formation of intransitive verbs:		
Past stem + -بوو- + Personal ending		
Preverb (-نە) + Past stem + -بوو- + Personal ending		
Example: گەڕان - *to search*		Verb stem: -گەڕا-
Conjugation	من گەڕابووم.	I had searched
	تۆ گەڕابوویت.	You had searched
	ئەو گەڕابوو.	He/She/It had searched
	ئێمە گەڕابووین.	We had searched
	ئێوە گەڕابوون.	You had searched
	ئەوان گەڕابوون.	They had searched
Negation نە - not	من نەگەڕابووم.	I had **not** searched
	تۆ نەگەڕابوویت.	You had **not** searched
	ئەو نەگەڕابوو.	He/She/It had **not** searched
	ئێمە نەگەڕابووین.	We had **not** searched
	ئێوە نەگەڕابوون.	You had **not** searched
	ئەوان نەگەڕابوون.	They had **not** searched
Interrogative Can be formed with or without ئایا	من گەڕابووم؟	Had I searched?
	تۆ گەڕابوویت؟	Had you searched?
	ئەو گەڕابوو؟	Had he/she/it searched?
	ئێمە گەڕابووین؟	Had we searched?
	ئێوە گەڕابوون؟	Had you searched?
	ئەوان گەڕابوون؟	Had they searched?
	من نەگەڕابووم؟	Had I not searched?
	تۆ نەگەڕابوویت؟	Had you not searched?

THE PAST TENSES 44

Interrogative + Negation Can be formed with or without ئایا	ئەو نەگەڕابوو؟	Had he/she/it not searched?
	ئێمە نەگەڕابووین؟	Had we not searched?
	ئێوە نەگەڕابوون؟	Had you not searched?
	ئەوان نەگەڕابوون؟	Had they not searched?

Formation of separable compound verbs:
Past stem + Personal ending + -بوو- + Personal ending
Preverb (نە-) + Past stem + -بوو- + Personal ending

Example: دانیشتن - *to sit (down)*		Verb stem: -دانیشت-
Conjugation	من دانیشتبووم.	I had sat down
	تۆ دانیشتبوویت.	You had sat down
	ئەو دانیشتبوو.	He/She/It had sat down
	ئێمە دانیشتبووین.	We had sat down
	ئێوە دانیشتبوون.	You had sat down
	ئەوان دانیشتبوون.	They had sat down
Negation نە - *not*	من دانەنیشتبووم.	I had **not** sat down
	تۆ دانەنیشتبوویت.	You had **not** sat down
	ئەو دانەنیشتبوو.	He/She/It had **not** sat down
	ئێمە دانەنیشتبووین.	We had **not** sat down
	ئێوە دانەنیشتبوون.	You had **not** sat down
	ئەوان دانەنیشتبوون.	They had **not** sat down
Interrogative Can be formed with or without ئایا	من دانیشتبووم؟	Had I sat down?
	تۆ دانیشتبوویت؟	Had you sat down?
	ئەو دانیشتبوو؟	Had he/she/it sat down?
	ئێمە دانیشتبووین؟	Had we sat down?
	ئێوە دانیشتبوون؟	Had you sat down?

THE PAST TENSES

	ئەوان دانیشتبوون؟	Had they sat down?
Interrogative + Negation Can be formed with or without ئایا	دانەنیشتبووم؟	Had I not sat down?
	دانەنیشتبوویت؟	Had you not sat down?
	دانەنیشتبوو؟	Had he/she/it not sat down?
	دانەنیشتبووین؟	Had we not sat down?
	دانەنیشتبوون؟	Had you not sat down?
	دانەنیشتبوون؟	Had they not sat down?

Formation of separable compound verbs with the suffix -ەوە :

Past stem + -بوو- + Personal ending + -ەوە

Preverb (نە-) + Past stem + -بوو- + Personal ending + -ەوە

Example: گەڕانەوە - *to return*	Verb stem: گەڕا-..-ەوە	
Conjugation	من گەڕابوومەوە.	I had returned
	تۆ گەڕابوویتەوە.	You had returned
	ئەو گەڕابوویەوە.	He/She/It had returned
	ئێمە گەڕابووینەوە.	We had returned
	ئێوە گەڕابوونەوە.	You had returned
	ئەوان گەڕابوونەوە.	They had returned
Negation نە - not	نەگەڕابوومەوە.	I had **not** returned
	نەگەڕابوویتەوە.	You had **not** returned
	نەگەڕابوویەوە.	He/She/It had **not** returned
	نەگەڕابووینەوە.	We had **not** returned
	نەگەڕابوونەوە.	You had **not** returned
	نەگەڕابوونەوە.	They had **not** returned
Interrogative Can be formed with or without ئایا	گەڕابوومەوە؟	Had I returned?
	گەڕابوویتەوە؟	Had you returned?
	گەڕابوویەوە؟	Had he/she/it returned?
	گەڕابووینەوە؟	Had we returned?

THE PAST TENSES

	گەڕابوونەوە؟	Had you returned?
	گەڕابوونەوە؟	Had they returned?
Interrogative + Negation Can be formed with or without ئایا	نەگەڕابوومەوە؟	Had I not returned?
	نەگەڕابووىتەوە؟	Had you not returned?
	نەگەڕابوویەوە؟	Had he/she/it not returned?
	نەگەڕابووىنەوە؟	Had we not returned?
	نەگەڕابوونەوە؟	Had you not returned?
	نەگەڕابوونەوە؟	Had they not returned?

Formation of transitive verbs:

Past stem + -بوو- + Personal ending

Preverb (-نە) + Personal ending + Past stem + -بوو-

Example: بینین - *to see*		Verb stem: -بینی-
Conjugation **without object**	من بینیبووم.	I had seen
	تۆ بینیبووت.	You had seen
	ئەو بینیبووی.	He/She had seen
	ئێمە بینیبوومان.	We had seen
	ئێوە بینیبووتان.	You had seen
	ئەوان بینیبوویان.	They had seen
Negation نە - **not**	من نەمبینیبوو.	I had **not** seen
	تۆ نەتبینیبوو.	You had **not** seen
	ئەو نەیبینیبوو.	He/She/It had **not** seen
	ئێمە نەمانبینیبوو.	We had **not** seen
	ئێوە نەتانبینیبوو.	You had **not** seen
	ئەوان نەیانبینیبوو.	They had **not** seen
Interrogative	من بینیبووم؟	Had I seen?
	تۆ بینیبووت؟	Had you seen?
	ئەو بینیبووی؟	Had he/she/it seen?
	ئێمە بینیبوومان؟	Had we seen?
	ئێوە بینیبووتان؟	Had you seen?

THE PAST TENSES

	ئەوان بینیوویان؟	Had they seen?
Interrogative + Negation	من نەمبینیبوو؟	Had I not seen?
	تۆ نەتبینیبوو؟	Had you not seen?
	ئەو نەیبینیبوو؟	Had he/she/it not seen?
	ئێمە نەمانبینیبوو؟	Had we not seen?
	ئێوە نەتانبینیبوو؟	Had you not seen?
	ئەوان نەیانبینیبوو؟	Had they not seen?

Formation of transitive verbs „with an object"		
Object + Personal ending of Subject & Past stem + -بوو		
Object + P. ending of Subject & Preverb (-نە) + Past stem + -بوو		
Example: بینین - *to see*		Verb stem: -بینی-
Conjugation with object	من تۆم بینیبوو.	I had seen you.
	تۆ منت بینیبوو.	You had seen me.
	ئەو ئەوی بینیبوو.	He/She had seen her/him.
	ئەو ئێمەی بینیبوو.	He/She had seen us.
	ئێمە ئێوەمان بینیبوو.	We had seen you
	ئێوە ئەوانتان بینیبوو.	You had seen them.
	ئەوان منیان بینیبوو.	They had seen me.
Negation نە – *not* No difference **with** or **without** pronouns	تۆم نەبینیبوو.	I had **not** seen you.
	منت نەبینیبوو.	You had **not** seen me.
	ئەوی نەبینیبوو.	He/she had **not** seen her/him.
	ئێمەی نەبینیبوو.	He/She had **not** seen us.
	ئێوەمان نەبینیبوو.	We had **not** seen you
	ئەوانتان نەبینیبوو.	You had **not** seen them.
	منیان نەبینیبوو.	They had **not** seen me.
Interrogative	تۆم بینیبوو؟	Had I seen you?
	منت بینیبوو؟	Had you seen me?
	ئەوی بینیبوو؟	Had he seen her/him?

THE PAST TENSES

Can be formed with or without ئایا	ئێمەی بینیبوو؟	Had she seen us?
	ئێوەمان بینیبوو؟	Had we seen you?
	ئەوانتان بینیبوو؟	Had you seen them?
	منیان بینیبوو؟	Had they seen me?
Interrogative + Negation Can be formed with or without ئایا	تۆم نەبینیبوو؟	Had I not seen you?
	منت نەبینیبوو؟	Had you not seen me?
	ئەوی نەبینیبوو؟	Had he not seen her/him?
	ئێمەی نەبینیبوو؟	Had she not seen us?
	ئێوەمان نەبینیبوو؟	Had we not seen you?
	ئەوانتان نەبینیبوو؟	Had you not seen them?
	منیان نەبینیبوو؟	Had they not seen me?

More Examples

پێنووسەکەم دابوو بە کچەکە.	I had given the pen to the girl.
پێنووسەکەت دابوو بە کچەکە.	You had given the pen to the girl.
پێنووسەکەی دابوو بە کچەکە.	He/She had given the pen to the girl.
پێنووسەکەمان دابوو بە کچەکە.	We had given the pen to the girl.
پێنووسەکەتان دابوو بە کچەکە.	You had given the pen to the girl.
پێنووسەکەیان دابوو بە کچەکە.	They had given the pen to the girl
پێنووسەکەم نەدابوو بە کچەکە.	I hadn't given the pen to the girl.
پێنووسەکەت نەدابوو بە کچەکە.	You hadn't given the pen to the girl.
پێنووسەکەی نەدابوو بە کچەکە.	He/She hadn't given the pen to the girl.
پێنووسەکەمان نەدابوو بە کچەکە	We hadn't given the pen to the girl
پێنووسەکەتان نەدابوو بە کچەکە.	You hadn't given the pen to the girl.
پێنووسەکەیان نەدابوو بە کچەکە.	They hadn't given the pen to the girl.

The Present Perfect Tense

This tense is used for actions in the past that still affect the present.

Formation of intransitive verbs with a stem ending in a consonant:		
Past stem + -وو- + Personal ending + -ه		
Preverb (نه-) + Past stem + -وو- + Personal ending + -ه		
Example: هاتن - *to come*		Verb stem: -هات-
Conjugation	من هاتوومه.	I have come. (**still there**)
	تۆ هاتوویته.	You have come.
	ئهو هاتووه.	He/She/It has come.
	ئێمه هاتووینه.	We have come.
	ئێوه هاتوونه.	You have come.
	ئهوان هاتوونه.	They have come.
Negation نه - *not*	من نههاتوومه.	I have **not** come.
	تۆ نههاتوویت.	You have **not** come.
	ئهو نههاتووه.	He/She/It has **not** come.
	ئێمه نههاتووینه.	We have **not** come.
	ئێوه نههاتوونه.	You have **not** come.
	ئهوان نههاتوونه.	They have **not** come.
Interrogative Can be formed with or without ئایا	من هاتوومه؟	Have I come?
	تۆ هاتوویته؟	Have you come?
	ئهو هاتووه؟	Has he/she/it come?
	ئێمه هاتووینه؟	Have we come?
	ئێوه هاتوونه؟	Have you come?
	ئهوان هاتوونه؟	Have they come?
Interrogative + Negation Can be formed with or without ئایا	من نههاتوومه؟	Have I not come?
	تۆ نههاتوویت؟	Have you not come?
	ئهو نههاتووه؟	Has he/she/it not come?
	ئێمه نههاتووینه؟	Have we not come?
	ئێوه نههاتوونه؟	Have you not come?
	ئهوان نههاتوونه؟	Have they not come?

THE PAST TENSES

Formation of intransitive verbs with a stem ending in a vowel:
Past stem + -و- + Personal ending + -ه
Preverb (نه-) + Past stem + -و- + Personal ending + -ه

| Example: گەڕان - *to search* | Verb stem: -گەڕا- |

Conjugation	من گەڕاومە.	I have searched. (happened already/before)
	تۆ گەڕاویتە.	You have searched.
	ئەو گەڕاوە.	He/She/It has searched.
	ئێمە گەڕاوینە.	We have searched.
	ئێوە گەڕاونە.	You have searched.
	ئەوان گەڕاونە.	They have searched.
Negation نە - *not*	نەگەڕاومە.	I have **not** searched.
	نەگەڕاویتە.	You have **not** searched.
	نەگەڕاوە.	He/She/It has **not** searched.
	نەگەڕاوینە.	We have **not** searched.
	نەگەڕاونە.	You have **not** searched.
	نەگەڕاونە.	They have **not** searched.
Interrogative Can be formed with or without ئایا	من گەڕاومە؟	Have I searched?
	تۆ گەڕاویتە؟	Have you searched?
	ئەو گەڕاوە؟	Has he/she/it searched?
	ئێمە گەڕاوینە؟	Have we searched?
	ئێوە گەڕاونە؟	Have you searched?
	ئەوان گەڕاونە؟	Have they searched?
Interrogative + Negation Can be formed with or without ئایا	نەگەڕاومە؟	Have I not searched?
	نەگەڕاویتە؟	Have you not searched?
	نەگەڕاوە؟	Has he/she/it not searched?
	نەگەڕاوینە؟	Have we not searched?
	نەگەڕاونە؟	Have you not searched?
	نەگەڕاونە؟	Have they not searched?

The ending ه- is sometimes being neglected. **e.g.:**
من گەڕاوم = *I've searched*   من هاتووم = *I've come*

THE PAST TENSES

Formation of intransitive verbs with a stem ending in a consonant:		
Prefix + Past stem + -وو- + Personal ending + -ە		
Prefix + Preverb (نە-) + Past stem + -وو- + Personal ending + -ە		
Example: دانیشتن - *to sit (down)*		Verb stem: -دانیشت-
Conjugation	من دانیشتوومە.	I've sat down.
	تۆ دانیشتوویتە.	You've sat down.
	ئەو دانیشتوووە.	He/She/It has sat down
	ئێمە دانیشتووینە.	We've sat down.
	ئێوە دانیشتوونە.	You've sat down.
	ئەوان دانیشتوونە.	They've sat down.
Negation نە - not	من دانەنیشتوومە.	I've **not** sat down.
	تۆ دانەنیشتوویت.	You've **not** sat down.
	ئەو دانەنیشتوووە.	He/She/It has **not** sat down.
	ئێمە دانەنیشتووینە.	We've **not** sat down.
	ئێوە دانەنیشتوونە.	You've **not** sat down.
	ئەوان دانەنیشتوونە.	They've **not** sat down.
Interrogative Can be formed with or without ئایا	من دانیشتوومە؟	Have I sat down?
	تۆ دانیشتوویتە؟	Have you sat down?
	ئەو دانیشتوووە؟	Has he/she sat down?
	ئێمە دانیشتووینە؟	Have we sat down?
	ئێوە دانیشتوونە؟	Have you sat down?
	ئەوان دانیشتوونە؟	Have they sat down?
Interrogative + Negation Can be formed with or without ئایا	من دانەنیشتوومە؟	Have I not sat down?
	تۆ دانەنیشتوویتە؟	Have you not sat down?
	ئەو دانەنیشتوووە؟	Has he/she not sat down?
	ئێمە دانەنیشتووینە؟	Have we not sat down?
	ئێوە دانەنیشتوونە؟	Have you not sat down?

THE PAST TENSES

	ئەوان دانەنیشتوونە؟	Have they not sat down?

 The ending -وو- is often shortened to -و- in everyday life.
e.g.: من دانیشتوومە= من دانیشتووومە = *I've sat down.*

Formation of separable compound verbs with the suffix -ەوە :
Past stem + -و- + Personal ending + -ـتـ- + -ەوە-
Preverb (-نە) + Past stem + -و- + Personal ending + -ـتـ- + -ەوە-

Example: گەڕانەوە - *to return*	Verb stem: گەڕا-...-ەوە

Conjugation	گەڕاومەتەوە.	I have returned. (happened already & there)
	گەڕاویتەوە.	You have returned.
	گەڕاوەتەوە.	He/She/It has returned.
	گەڕاوینەتەوە.	We have returned.
	گەڕاونەتەوە.	You have returned.
	گەڕاونەتەوە.	They have returned.
Negation نە - not	نەگەڕاومەتەوە.	I have **not** returned.
	نەگەڕاویتەوە.	You have **not** returned.
	نەگەڕاوەتەوە.	He/ returned /It has **not** returned.
	نەگەڕاوینەتەوە.	We have **not** returned.
	نەگەڕاونەتەوە.	You have **not** returned.
	نەگەڕاونەتەوە.	They have **not** returned.
Interrogative Can be formed with or without ئایا	گەڕاومەتەوە؟	Have I returned?
	گەڕاویتەوە؟	Have you returned?
	گەڕاوەتەوە؟	Has he/she/it returned?
	گەڕاوینەتەوە؟	Have we returned?
	گەڕاونەتەوە؟	Have you returned?
	گەڕاونەتەوە؟	Have they returned?
Interrogative + Negation	نەگەڕاومەتەوە؟	Have I not returned?
	نەگەڕاویتەوە؟	Have you not returned?
	نەگەڕاوەتەوە؟.	Has he/she/it not returned?

THE PAST TENSES

Can be formed with or without ئایا	نەگەڕاوینەتەوە؟	Have we not returned?
	نەگەڕاونەتەوە؟	Have you not returned?
	نەگەڕاونەتەوە؟	Have they not returned?

 Second person singular گەڕاویتەوە doesn't get the suffix -ـت.

Formation of transitive verbs with a stem ending in a vowel:		
Past stem + -و- + Personal ending + -ە		
Preverb (-نە) + Personal ending + Past stem + -وە		
Example: بینین - *to see*		Verb stem: -بینی-

Conjugation **without object**	من بینیومە.	I've seen. (happened already)
	تۆ بینیوتە.	You have seen.
	ئەو بینیویەتی.	He has seen.
	ئێمە بینیومانە.	We have seen.
	ئێوە بینیوتانە.	You have seen.
	ئەوان بینیویانە.	They have seen.
Negation **نە - not**	من نەمبینیوە.	I have **not** seen.
	تۆ نەتبینیوە.	You have **not** seen.
	ئەو نەیبینیوە.	He has **not** seen.
	ئێمە نەمانبینیوە.	We have **not** seen.
	ئێوە نەتانبینیوە.	You have **not** seen.
	ئەوان نەیانبینیوە.	They have **not** seen.
Interrogative	من بینیومە؟	Have I seen?
	تۆ بینیوتە؟	Have you seen?
	ئەو بینیویەتی؟	Has he/she seen?
	ئێمە بینیومانە؟	Have we seen?
	ئێوە بینیوتانە؟	Have you seen?
	ئەوان بینیویانە؟	Have they seen?
	من نەمبینیوە؟	Have I not seen?
	تۆ نەتبینیوە؟	Have you not seen?

THE PAST TENSES

Interrogative + Negation	ئەو نەيبينيوە؟	Has he/she not seen?
	ئێمە نەمانبينيوە؟	Have we not seen?
	ئێوە نەتانبينيوە؟	Have you not seen?
	ئەوان نەيانبينيوە؟	Have they not seen?

 The ending of the 3rd person sg. is an exception: تی or یەتی
Alternative conjugation: ئەو بينيويەتی = ئەو بينيوێتی

Formation of transitive verbs „with an object"
Object + Personal ending & Past stem + -وە
Object + Personal ending & Preverb (-نە) + Past stem + -وە

Example: بينين - *to see*		Verb stem: -بينی
Conjugation with object	تۆم بينيوە.	I've seen you. (**happened already, person is known**)
	منت بينيوە.	You've seen me.
	ئەوی بينيوە.	He/She has seen her/him.
	ئێمەی بينيوە.	He/She has seen us.
	ئێوەمان بينيوە.	We have seen you
	ئەوانتان بينيوە.	You have seen them.
	منيان بينيوە.	They have seen me.
Negation نە - *not*	تۆم نەبينيوە.	I have **not** seen you.
	منت نەبينيوە.	You've **not** seen me.
	ئەوی نەبينيوە.	He/she has **not** seen her/him.
	ئێمەی نەبينيوە.	He/She has **not** seen us.
	ئێوەمان نەبينيوە.	We have **not** seen you
	ئەوانتان نەبينيوە.	You have **not** seen them.
	منيان نەبينيوە.	They have **not** seen me.

Interrogative Can be formed with or without ئایا	تۆم بینیوه؟	Have I seen you?
	منت بینیوه؟	Have you seen me?
	ئەوی بینیوه؟	Has he seen her/him?
	ئێمەی بینیوه؟	Has she seen us?
	ئێوەمان بینیوه؟	Have we seen you?
	ئەوانتان بینیوه؟	Have you seen them?
	منیان بینیوه؟	Have they seen me?
Interrogative + Negation Can be formed with or without ئایا	تۆم نەبینیوه؟	Have I not seen you?
	منت نەبینیوه؟	Have you not seen me?
	ئەوی نەبینیوه؟	Has he not seen her/him?
	ئێمەی نەبینیوه؟	Has she not seen us?
	ئێوەمان نەبینیوه؟	Have we not seen you?
	ئەوانتان نەبینیوه؟	Have you not seen them?
	منیان نەبینیوه؟	Have they not seen me?

More Examples

من سێوێکم بینیوه.	I've seen an apple.
من دوو سێوم بینیوه.	I've seen two apples.
من سێوەکەم بینیوه.	I've seen the apple.
من هیچ سێوێکم نەبینیوه.	I've **not** seen an apple.
من سێوەکانم نەبینیوه.	I've **not** seen apples.

پێنووسەکەم داوه بە کچەکە.	I've given the pen to the girl.
پێنووسەکەت داوه بە کچەکە.	You've given the pen to the girl.
پێنووسەکەی داوه بە کچەکە.	He/She has given the pen to the girl.
پێنووسەکەمان داوه بە کچەکە.	We've given the pen to the girl.
پێنووسەکەتان داوه بە کچەکە.	You've given the pen to the girl.
پێنووسەکەیان داوه بە کچەکە.	They've given the pen to the girl.

THE FUTURE TENSE

Both Present and Future tenses are the same in Sorani. To make it clear that the action is going to be taken in the future, time words: (tomorrow = سبەی/بەیانی, day after tomorrow = دو سبەی/بەیانی, later = دواتر, next week/month = هەفتەی/مانگی داهاتوو) are used.

Formation of regular verbs:

Preverb (دە-) + Present stem + Personal ending
Preverb (نا-) + Present stem + Personal ending

Example: چوون - *to go*		Verb stem: -چ-
Conjugation	من دەچم.	I go/**will** go.
	تۆ دەچیت.	You go/**will** go.
	ئەو دەچێت.	He/She/It goes/**will** go.
	ئێمە دەچین.	We go/**will** go.
	ئێوە دەچن.	You go/**will** go.
	ئەوان دەچن.	They go/**will** go.
Negation (نا instead of دە) نا - not	من ناچم.	I **won't** go.
	تۆ ناچیت.	You **won't** go.
	ئەو ناچێت.	He/She/It **won't** go.
	ئێمە ناچین.	We **won't** go.
	ئێوە ناچن.	You **won't** go.
	ئەوان ناچن.	They **won't** go.
Conjugation with a time word	من بەیانی دەچم.	I **will** go tomorrow/in the morning.
	تۆ بەیانی دەچیت.	You go/**will** go tomorrow/in the morning.
	ئەو بەیانی دەچێت.	He/She/It goes/**will** go tomorrow/in the morning.
	ئێمە بەیانی دەچین.	We go/**will** go tomorrow/in the morning.
	ئێوە بەیانی دەچن.	You go/**will** go tomorrow/in the morning.
	ئەوان بەیانی دەچن.	They go/**will** go tomorrow/in the morning.

THE SUBJUNCTIVE

The Subjunctive (Present Tense)

Formation of the verb „to be" in the Present Tense:		
Present stem + Personal ending		
Preverb (نە) & Subject & Present stem + Personal ending		
Example: بوون - *to be*		Verb stem: -ب-
Conjugation	من بم	(If) I were
	تۆ بيت	(If) you were
	ئەو بێت	(If) he/she/it were
	ئێمە بين	(If) we were
	ئێوە بن	(If) you were
	ئەوان بن	(If) they were
Negation نە - *not*	گەر من نە بم	If I were **not**,
	گەر تۆ نە بيت	If you were **not**,
	گەر ئەو نە بێت	If he/she/it were **not**,
	گەر ئێمە نە بين	If we were **not**,
	گەر ئێوە نە بن	If you were **not**,
	گەر ئەوان نە بن	If they were **not**,

 The Sorani word ئەگەر or گەر which means „if" is not obligatory. من بم or ئەگەر من بم means „**If I were**"

More Examples

ئەگەر هەستم، دەبينيت چەند درێژم	If I should stand up, you'll see how tall I am
ئەگەر ئەوان دەست پێ بکەن، ناتوانن بوەستن.	If they were to start, they could not stop.
ئەگەر ئاو نەخواتەوە، بە تينوێتی دەمێنێتەوە.	If he were not to drink, he'd remain thirsty.
ئەگەر ئەو نەيێت، منيش ناچم.	If he should not come, I won't go either.

The Subjunctive (Conditional perfect)

The subjunctive in the conditional perfect expresses that actions (wishes, ideas or speculations) are no longer realizable.

Formation of the verb „to be/become" in Conditional perfect:
-ب + Past stem + Personal ending + -ايه
-نه + Past stem + Personal ending + -ايه

Example: بوون – *to be/become*		Verb stem: -بوو
Conjugation	من ببوومايه	(If) I would have become
	تۆ ببوويتايه	(If) you would have become
	ئهو ببوووايه	(If) he/she/it would have become
	ئێمه ببووينايه	(If) we would have become
	ئێوه ببووناىه	(If) you would have become
	ئهوان ببووناىه	(If) they would have become
Negation نه - not	من نهبوومايه	(If) I would **not** have become
	تۆ نهبوويتايه	(If) you would **not** have become
	ئهو نهبوووايه	(If) he/she/it would **not** have become
	ئێمه نهبووينايه	(If) we would **not** have become
	ئێوه نهبووناىه	(If) you would **not** have become
	ئهوان نهبووناىه	(If) they would **not** have become

من ببوومايه مامۆستا - *(If) I would have become a teacher*

In some regions of Kurdistan **تهببوومايه** is used instead of **ببوومايه**.

THE SUBJUNCTIVE

Formation of intransitive verbs: Form I	
ب- + Past stem + -بایه- + Personal ending	
نه- + Past stem + -بایه- + Personal ending	
Example: ڕۆیشتن - *to go*	Verb stem: -ڕۆشت-

Conjugation	ئەگەر بڕۆشتبایەم	(If) I would have gone
	ئەگەر بڕۆشتبایەی	(If) you would have gone
	ئەگەر بڕۆشتبایە	(If) he/she/it would have gone
	ئەگەر بڕۆشتبایەن	(If) we would have gone
	ئەگەر بڕۆشتبایەن	(If) you would have gone
	ئەگەر بڕۆشتبایەن	(If) they would have gone
Negation **نه - not**	من نەڕۆشتبایەم	(If) I would **not** have gone
	تۆ نەڕۆشتبایەی	(If) you would **not** have gone
	ئەو نەڕۆشتبایە	(If) he/she/it would **not** have gone
	ئێمە نەڕۆشتبایەن	(If) we would **not** have gone
	ئێوە نەڕۆشتبایەن	(If) you would **not** have gone
	ئەوان نەڕۆشتبایەن	(If) they would **not** have gone

 In some regions of Kurdistan ئەگەر من بڕۆشتمایە is used instead of ئەگەر من بڕۆشتبایەم.

THE SUBJUNCTIVE

Formation of intransitive verbs: Form II

-ن + Past stem + Personal ending + ايه-
Preverb (نه-) + Past stem + Personal ending + ايه-

Example: رۆیشتن - *to go*		Verb stem: -ڕۆیشت
Conjugation	من بڕۆیشتمایه	(If) I would have gone
	تۆ بڕۆیشتیتایه	(If) you would have gone
	ئهو بڕۆیشتایه	(If) he/she/it would have gone
	ئێمه بڕۆیشتینایه	(If) we would have gone
	ئێوه بڕۆیشتنایه	(If) you would have gone
	ئهوان بڕۆیشتنایه	(If) they would have gone
Negation نه - not	من نهڕۆیشتمایه	(If) I would **not** have gone
	تۆ نهڕۆیشتیتایه	(If) you would **not** have gone
	ئهو نهڕۆیشتایه	(If) he/she/it would **not** have gone
	ئێمه نهڕۆیشتینایه	(If) we would **not** have gone
	ئێوه نهڕۆیشتنایه	(If) you would **not** have gone
	ئهوان نهڕۆیشتنایه	(If) they would **not** have gone

Formation of separable compound verbs with the suffix -هوه:

-ب + Verb stem + -(يه)با + Personal ending + هوه-
-نه + Verb stem + -(يه)با + Personal ending + هوه-

Example: گهڕانهوه - *to return*		Verb stem: -گهڕا-...-هوه
Conjugation	من بگهڕایهمهوه	(If) I would have returned
	تۆ بگهڕایتایهوه	(If) you would have returned
	ئهو بگهڕابایهوه	(If) he/she/it would have returned

THE SUBJUNCTIVE

	ئێمە بگەڕاباینەوە	(If) we would have returned
	ئێوە بگەڕابانەوە	(If) you would have returned
	ئەوان بگەڕابانەوە	(If) they would have returned
Negation (نە instead of ب) نە - not	من نەگەڕایەمەوە	(If) I would **not** have returned
	تۆ نەگەڕایتایەوە	(If) you would **not** have returned
	ئەو نەگەڕابایەوە	(If) he/she/it would **not** have returned
	ئێمە نەگەڕاباینەوە	(If) we would **not** have returned
	ئێوە نەگەڕابانەوە	(If) you would **not** have returned
	ئەوان نەگەڕابانەوە	(If) they would **not** have returned

 The short form of -با(يە)- is being used:
ئەگەر بگەڕایەمەوە = ئەگەر بگەڕابایەمەوە

Formation of transitive verbs:
-ب + Personal ending + Verb stem + ـایە-
-نە + Personal ending + Verb stem + ـایە-

Example: بینین - *to see*	Verb stem: -بین-	
Conjugation	من بمبینایە	(If) I would have seen
	تۆ بتبینایە	(If) you would have seen
	ئەو بیبینایە	(If) he/she/it would have seen
	ئێمە بمانبینایە	(If) we would have seen
	ئێوە بتانبینایە	(If) you would have seen
	ئەوان بیانبینایە	(If) they would have seen
	من نەمبینایە	(If) I would **not** have seen

THE SUBJUNCTIVE

Negation (نه instead of ب)	تۆ نەتبینیایە	(If) you would **not** have seen
	ئەو نەیبینایە	(If) he/she/it would **not** have seen
نه - not	ئێمە نەمانبینیایە	(If) we would **not** have seen
	ئێوە نەتانبینیایە	(If) you would **not** have seen
	ئەوان نەیانبینیایە	(If) they would **not** have seen

 The word ئەگەر or گەر which means „**if**" is not obligatory.
Alternative conjugation: ئەگەر من بمبینابا = *If I would have seen*

The Subjunctive (Simple Past & Pluperfect Tenses)

The subjunctive in the past tense expresses a personal statement.

Formation of the verb „to be":	
Past stem + Personal ending + ـایە	
Preverb (نە) + Past stem + Personal ending + ـایە	
Example: بوون – *to be*	Verb stem: بوو-

Conjugation	من بوومایە	(If) I were
	تۆ بوویتایە	(If) you were
	ئەو بوووایە	(If) he/she/it were
	ئێمە بوونیایە	(If) we were
	ئێوە بوونایە	(If) you were
	ئەوان بوونایە	(If) they were
Negation نه - not	من نەبوومایە	(If) I were **not**
	تۆ نەبوویتایە	(If) you were **not**
	ئەو نەبوووایە	(If) he/she/it were **not**
	ئێمە نەبوونیایە	(If) we were **not**
	ئێوە نەبوونایە	(If) you were **not**
	ئەوان نەبوونایە	(If) they were **not**

 The word ئەگەر or گەر which means „**if**" is not obligatory.
Alternative translation: ئەگەر من بوومایە = *If I were*

THE SUBJUNCTIVE

Formation of intransitive verbs:	
Preverb (-ب) + Past stem + Personal ending + ـيه	
Preverb (نه-) + Past stem + Personal ending + ـيه	
Example: هاتن - *to come*	Verb stem: -هات-

Conjugation	من بهاتبام	(If) I had come
	تۆ بهاتبای	(If) you had come
	ئەو بهاتبا	(If) he/she/it had come
	ئێمە بهاتباین	(If) we had come
	ئێوە بهاتبان	(If) you had come
	ئەوان بهاتبان	(If) they had come
Negation ‌نه - not	من نەهاتبام	(If) I had **not** come
	تۆ نەهاتبای	(If) you had **not** come
	ئەو نەهاتبا	(If) he/she/it had **not** come
	ئێمە نەهاتباین	(If) we had **not** come
	ئێوە نەهاتبان	(If) you had **not** come
	ئەوان نەهاتبان	(If) they had **not** come

 In some regions of Kurdistan من بهاتبام is used instead of من بهاتمایه.

Formation of intransitive verbs:	
Preverb (-ب) + Past stem + Personal ending + ـایه	
Preverb (نه-) + Past stem + Personal ending + ـایه	
Example: هاتن - *to come*	Verb stem: -هات-

Conjugation	من بهاتمایه	(If) I had come
	تۆ بهاتیتایه	(If) you had come
	ئەو بهاتایه	(If) he/she/it had come
	ئێمە بهاتینایه	(If) we had come
	ئێوە بهاتنایه	(If) you had come
	ئەوان بهاتنایه	(If) they had come

THE SUBJUNCTIVE

Negation نه - not	من نەھاتمایە	(If) hadn't come
	تۆ نەھاتیتایە	(If) you hadn't come
	ئەو نەھاتایە	(If) he/she/it hadn't come
	ئێمە نەھاتیناىە	(If) we hadn't come
	ئێوە نەھاتنایە	(If) you hadn't come
	ئەوان نەھاتنایە	(If) they hadn't come

Formation of transitive verbs:

Preverb (ب-) + Personal ending + Past stem + ـایە

Preverb (نە-) + Personal ending + Past stem + ـایە

Example: خواردن – *to eat*		Verb stem: -خوارد-
Conjugation	من بمخواردایە	(If) I had eaten
	تۆ بتخواردایە	(If) you had eaten
	ئەو بیخواردایە	(If) he/she/it had eaten
	ئێمە بمانخواردایە	(If) we had eaten
	ئێوە بتانخواردایە	(If) you had eaten
	ئەوان بیانخواردایە	(If) they had eaten
Negation نه - not	من نەمخواردایە	(If) I had **not** eaten
	تۆ نەتخواردایە	(If) you had **not** eaten
	ئەو نەخواردایە	(If) he/she/it had **not** eaten
	ئێمە نەمانخواردایە	(If) we had **not** eaten
	ئێوە نەتانخواردایە	(If) you had **not** eaten
	ئەوان نەیانخواردایە	(If) they had **not** eaten

من بمخواردایە = بمخواردایە = ئەگەر بمخواردایە

Conditional Clauses

ئەگەر من تۆ بووبامایە، ئەم ئاوەم نەدەخواردە.   *If I were you, I would not have drunk this water.*
ئەگەر من بھاتمایە، تۆم دەبینی.   *If I had come, I would have seen you.*
ئەگەر زیاتر ھەولمبدایە، دەبوومە مامۆستایەک.   *If I had studied well, I would have been a teacher.*
ئەگەر نانی ئێوارە بخۆم، بۆت دەنووسم.   *If I eat dinner, I will write you.*
ئەگەر من بمخواردایە، تۆ دەتزانی.   *If I have eaten it, you will see.*

 It's not obligatory to use ئەگەر „if" in Sorani conditional sentences.

The Irrealis (Past tenses)

The irrealis refers to unreal events. It describes an event that did not happen in the past and is therefore irretrievable.

Formation of the verb „to be/become" in the Pluperfect:	
Preverb (-دە) + Past stem + Personal ending	
Preverb (-نە) + Preverb (-دە) + Past stem + Personal ending	
Example: بوون – *to be/become*	Verb stem: -بوو-
Conjugation	من دەبووم	I would have been
	تۆ دەبوویت	You would have been
	ئەو دەبووە	He/She/It would have been
	ئێمە دەبووین	We would have been
	ئێوە دەبوون	You would have been
	ئەوان دەبوون	They would have been
Negation	من نەدەبووم	I would not have been
	تۆ نەدەبوویت	You would **not** have been
	ئەو نەدەبووە	He/She/It would **not** have been

THE SUBJUNCTIVE

نە – not	ئێمە نەدەبووین	We would **not** have been
	ئێوە نەدەبوون	You would **not** have been
	ئەوان نەدەبوون	They would **not** have been

 من دەبوومە مامۆستایەک – *I would have been a teacher.*
من سەرکەوتوو دەبووم – *I would have been successful.*

 من دەبوومە = من دەبووم both mean: I would have been

Formation of intransitive verbs:

Preverb (-دە) + Past stem + Personal ending

Preverb (-نە) + Preverb (-دە) + Past stem + Personal ending

Example: کەوتن – *to fall*		Verb stem: -کەوت
Conjugation	من دەکەوتم	I would have fallen
	تۆ دەکەوتیت	You would have fallen
	ئەو دەکەوت	He/She/It would have fallen
	ئێمە دەکەوتین	We would have fallen
	ئێوە دەکەوتن	You would have fallen
	ئەوان دەکەوتن	They would have fallen
Negation نە – not	من نەدەکەوتم	I would **not** have fallen
	تۆ نەدەکەوتیت	You would **not** have fallen
	ئەو نەدەکەوت	He/She/It would **not** have fallen
	ئێمە نەدەکەوتین	We would **not** have fallen
	ئێوە نەدەکەوتن	You would **not** have fallen
	ئەوان نەدەکەوتن	They would **not** have fallen

THE SUBJUNCTIVE

Formation of transitive verbs:		
Preverb (دە-) + Personal ending + Past stem		
Preverb (نە-) + Personal ending + Past stem		
Example: خواردن – *to eat*		Verb stem: -خوارد-
Conjugation	من دەمخوارد	I would have eaten
	تۆ دەتخوارد	You would have eaten
	ئەو دەیخوارد	He/She/It would have eaten
	ئێمە دەمانخوارد	We would have eaten
	ئێوە دەتانخوارد	You would have eaten
	ئەوان دەیانخوارد	They would have eaten
Negation نە – *not*	من نەمخوارد	I would **not** have eaten
	تۆ نەتخوارد	You would **not** have eaten
	ئەو نەیخوارد	He/She/It would **not** have eaten
	ئێمە نەمانخوارد	We would **not** have eaten
	ئێوە نەتانخوارد	You would **not** have eaten
	ئەوان نەیانخوارد	They would **not** have eaten

THE SUBJUNCTIVE

The Subjunctive with با

The word با cannot be translated directly but the meaning of با corresponds most closely to the word **should**. Depending on the context it implies a **desire**, a **condition** or an **order**. Therefore, we translate با as **let**, **want** or **should**.

Formation:	
با & Preverb (-ب) + Present stem + Personal ending	
با & Preverb (-نە) + Present stem + Personal ending	
Example: بینین – *to see*	Verb stem: -بین-
Conjugation	با ببینم	I want to see/Let me see
	با ببینیت	You should see
	با ببینێت	Let him/her see
	با ببینین	We should see/Let's see
	با ببینن	You should see
	با ببینن	Let them see
Negation نە – *not*	با نەبینم	I do **not** want to see
	با نەبینیت	You should **not** see
	با نەبینێت	Let him/her **not** see
	با نەبینین	We should **not** see
	با نەبینن	You should **not** ee
	با نەبینن	Let them **not** see

More Examples

با ببێت!	Let it be!	با نەبێت!	Let it **not** be!
با بچین!	Let's go!	با نەچین!	Let's **not** go!
با هەڵبژاردن نەکرێت			
The election should not take place. *(I don't want it to happen)*			

THE PASSIVE VOICE

The Passive Voice in the Present Tense

Formation in the Present Tense:		
Preverb (ده-) + Present stem + -رێ- + Personal ending		
Preverb (نا-) + Present stem + -رێ- + Personal ending		
Verb بینین - *to see*		
Conjugation	.من دەبینرێم	I'm being seen/I'm seen
	.تۆ دەبینرێیت	You are seen
	.ئەو دەبینرێت	He/She/It is seen
	.ئێمە دەبینرێین	We are seen
	.ئێوە دەبینرێن	You are seen
	.ئەوان دەبینرێن	They are seen
Negation (نا instead of ده) نا - *not*	.من نابینرێم	I'm being seen/I'm **not** seen
	.تۆ نابینرێیت	You are **not** seen
	.ئەو نابینرێت	He/She/It is **not** seen
	.ئێمە نابینرێین	We are **not** seen
	.ئێوە نابینرێن	You are **not** seen
	.ئەوان نابینرێن	They are **not** seen
Interrogative Can be formed with or without ئایا	من دەبینرێم؟	Am I seen?
	تۆ دەبینرێیت؟	Are you seen?
	ئەو دەبینرێت؟	Is he/she/it seen?
	ئێمە دەبینرێین؟	Are we seen?
	ئێوە دەبینرێن؟	Are you seen?
	ئەوان دەبینرێن؟	Are they seen?
Interrogative + Negation Can be formed with or without ئایا	من نابینرێم؟	Am I not seen?
	تۆ نابینرێیت؟	Are you not seen?
	ئەو نابینرێت؟	Is he/she/it not seen?
	ئێمە نابینرێین؟	Are we not seen?
	ئێوە نابینرێن؟	Are you not seen?
	ئەوان نابینرێن؟	Are they not seen?

The Passive Voice in the Simple Past Tense

	Formation in the Simple Past Tense:	
	Verb stem + -را- + Personal ending	
	Preverb (-نه) + Verb stem + -را- + Personal ending	
	Example: بینین - *to see*	Verb stem: -بین-
Conjugation	من بینرام.	I was seen
	تۆ بینرایت.	You were seen
	ئەو بینرا.	He/She/It was seen
	ئێمە بینراین.	We were seen
	ئێوە بینران.	You were seen
	ئەوان بینران.	They were seen
Negation نه - not	من نەبینرام.	I wasn't seen
	تۆ نەبینرایت	You weren't seen
	ئەو نەبینرا.	He/She/It wasn't seen
	ئێمە نەبینراین.	We weren't seen
	ئێوە نەبینران.	You weren't seen
	ئەوان نەبینران.	They weren't seen
Interrogative Can be formed with or without ئایا	من بینرام؟	Was I seen?
	تۆ بینرایت؟	Were you seen?
	ئەو بینرا؟	Was he/she/it seen?
	ئێمە بینراین؟	Were we seen?
	ئێوە بینران؟	Were you seen?
	ئەوان بینران؟	Were they seen?
Interrogative + Negation Can be formed with or without ئایا	من نەبینرام؟	Was I not seen?
	تۆ نەبینرایت؟	Were you seen?
	ئەو نەبینرا؟	Was he/she/it not seen?
	ئێمە نەبینراین؟	Were we not seen?
	ئێوە نەبینران؟	Were you not seen?
	ئەوان نەبینران؟	Were they not seen?

The Passive Voice in the Past Progressive Tense

Formation in the Past Progressive Tense:		
Preverb (دە-) + Present stem + -را- + Personal ending		
Preverb (نە-) + Present stem + -را- + Personal ending		
Example: بینین - *to see*		Verb stem: -بین-
Conjugation	من دەبینرام.	I was being seen.
	تۆ دەبینرایت.	You were being seen.
	ئەو دەبینرا.	He/She/It was being seen.
	ئێمە دەبینراین.	We were being seen.
	ئێوە دەبینران.	You were being seen.
	ئەوان دەبینران.	They were being seen.
Negation نە - *not*	نەدەبینرام.	I wasn't being seen.
	نەدەبینرایت.	You weren't being seen.
	نەدەبینرا.	He/She/It wasn't being seen.
	نەدەبینراین.	We weren't being seen.
	نەدەبینران.	You weren't being seen.
	نەدەبینران.	They weren't being seen.
Interrogative Can be formed with or without ئایا	من دەبینرام؟	Was I being seen?
	تۆ دەبینرایت؟	Were you being seen?
	ئەو دەبینرا؟	Was he/she/it being seen?
	ئێمە دەبینراین؟	Were we being seen?
	ئێوە دەبینران؟	Were you being seen?
	ئەوان دەبینران؟	Were they being seen?
Interrogative + Negation Can be formed with or without ئایا	من نەبینرام؟	Was I **not** being seen?
	تۆ نەبینرایت؟	Were you **not** being seen?
	ئەو نەبینرا؟	Was he/she/it **not** being seen?
	ئێمە نەبینراین؟	Were we **not** being seen?
	ئێوە نەبینران؟	Were you **not** being seen?
	ئەوان نەبینران؟	Were they **not** being seen?

The Passive Voice in the Present Perfect Tense

Formation in the Present Perfect Tense:		
Verb stem + -‫راو‬- + Personal ending		
Preverb (‫نه‬-) + Personal ending + Verb stem + -‫راو‬-		
Main verb ‫بینین‬ - *to see*		
Conjugation	‫من بینراوم.‬	I have been seen.
	‫تۆ بینراویت.‬	You have been seen.
	‫ئەو بینراویت.‬	He/she/It has been seen.
	‫ئێمە بینراوین.‬	We have been seen.
	‫ئێوە بینراون.‬	You have been seen.
	‫ئەوان بینراون.‬	They have been seen.
Negation ‫نه‬ - not	‫من نەمبینراو.‬	I have **not** been seen.
	‫تۆ نەتبینراو.‬	You have **not** been seen.
	‫ئەو نەیبینراو.‬	He/she/It has **not** been seen.
	‫ئێمە نەمانبینراو.‬	We have **not** been seen.
	‫ئێوە نەتانبینراو.‬	You have **not** been seen.
	‫ئەوان نەیانبینراو.‬	They have **not** been seen.
Interrogative Can be formed with or without ‫ئایا‬	‫من بینراوم؟‬	Have I been seen?
	‫تۆ بینراویت؟‬	Have you been seen?
	‫ئەو بینراویت؟‬	Has he/she/it been seen?
	‫ئێمە بینراوین؟‬	Have we been seen?
	‫ئێوە بینراون؟‬	Have you been seen?
	‫ئەوان بینراون؟‬	Have they been seen?
Interrogative + Negation Can be formed with or without ‫ئایا‬	‫نەمبینراو؟‬	Haven't I been seen?
	‫نەتبینراو؟‬	Haven't you been seen?
	‫نەیبینراو؟‬	Hasn't he/she/it been seen?
	‫نەمانبینراو؟‬	Haven't we been seen?
	‫نەتانبینراو؟‬	Haven't you been seen?
	‫نەیانبینراو؟‬	Haven't they been seen?

The Passive Voice in the Pluperfect Tense

Formation: Verb stem + رابوو + Personal ending Preverb (نه‌-) + Personal ending + Verb stem + رابوو		
Main verb بینین - *to see*		
Conjugation	من بینرابووم.	I had been seen.
	تۆ بینرابوویت.	You had been seen.
	ئەو بینرابوو.	He/She/It had been seen.
	ئێمە بینرابووین.	We had been seen.
	ئێوە بینرابوون.	You had been seen.
	ئەوان بینرابوون.	They had been seen.
Negation نه‌ - *not*	من نەمبینرابوو.	I had**n't** been seen.
	تۆ نەتبینرابوو.	You had**n't** been seen.
	ئەو نەیبینرابوو.	He/She/It had**n't** been seen.
	ئێمە نەمانبینرابوو.	We had**n't** been seen.
	ئێوە نەتانبینرابوو.	You had**n't** been seen.
	ئەوان نەیانبینرابوو.	They had**n't** been seen.
Interrogative Can be formed with or without ئایا	من بینرابووم؟	Had I been seen?
	تۆ بینرابوویت؟	Had you been seen?
	ئەو بینرابوو؟	Had he/she/it been seen?
	ئێمە بینرابووین؟	Had we been seen?
	ئێوە بینرابوون؟	Had you been seen?
	ئەوان بینرابوون؟	Had they been seen?
Interrogative + Negation Can be formed with or without ئایا	من نەمبینرابوو؟	Had I not been seen?
	تۆ نەتبینرابوو؟	Had you not been seen?
	ئەو نەیبینرابوو؟	Had he/she/it not been seen?
	ئێمە نەمانبینرابوو؟	Had we not been seen?
	ئێوە نەتانبینرابوو؟	Had you not been seen?
	ئەوان نەیانبینرابوو؟	Had they not been seen?

THE ADVERBS
1. The Most Common Temporal Adverbs

Adverb	Example
ئەمرۆ today	من ئەمرۆ دەرۆم. I am coming today.
دوێنێ yesterday	من دوێنێ هاتم. I came yesterday.
سبەی/بەیانی morning/tomorrow	من بەیانی دەچم. I will come tomorrow.
سبەیان/بەیانیان in the morning	من بەیانیان دێم. I come in the mornings.
لە نیوەڕۆ (at noon)	لە نیوەڕۆ دێمەوە. I'll come back at noon.
لە ئێوارەدا In the evening	لە ئێوارەدا دێمەوە. I come back in the evening.
لە شەودا at night	لە شەودا دێمەوە. I'm coming back at night.
ئێستا now	من ئێستا دێم. I am coming now.
دوایی/ دواتر later	دوایی دەچمە بازار. I'm going to bazaar later.
یەکسەر immediately	من یەکسەر دێم. I am coming immediately.
پێشتر in the past	من پێشتر دەهاتم. I used to come.
لە کاتێکی نێزیکدا soon	من لە کاتێکی نێزیکدا دێم. I will come soon.
هەندێ جار/ جار ندێ هە کات sometimes	هەندێ جار دەڵێم. I sometimes say.
هەمیشە/هەموو جار always	من هەمیشە دێم. I always come.
بە بەردەوامی regularly	من بە بەردەوامی هاتم. I came regularly.

THE ADVERBS

هەروو هەر often	من هەروو هەر هاتم. I often came.
کەم rarely/seldom	من کەم دێمە ماڵ. I rarely come home.
هیچ never	من هیچ نەهاتم. I never came.

2. The Most Common Modal Adverbs

Adverb	Example
بەراستی really	من بەراستی لێرەم. I am really here.
بەداخەوە / مخابن unfortunately	بەداخەوە من نارۆم. Unfortunately, I am not coming.
بەخۆشهاڵییەوە gladly	من بە خۆشهاڵییەوە دێم. I gladly come.
ڕەنگە maybe	ڕەنگە بێم. Maybe I come.
لە هەموو بارێکدا definitely	من لە هەموو بارێکدا لەوێم. I am definitely there.
ش- or یش- too, also; even	منیش. / تۆش. / من ئەوەشم پێت وتی. I even told you that. / You too. / Me too.
ئاوها / ئاوا like, so	ئەو ئاوا دیارە. It looks like that.
وەکو like, as	تۆ وەکو منی. You are like me.
تەواو thoroughly	من تەواو خاوێنی دەکەمەوە. I clean thoroughly.
هەمووویم / تەواو completely	من هەمووویم لە بیر کرد. I completely forgot it.
هێشتا still	من هێشتا لە ماڵەوەم. I am still at home.
پێکەوە together	ئێمە پێکەوە قسە دەکەین. We talk to each other.

3. The Most Common Local Adverbs

Adverb	Example
لێرە here	من لێرەم. I am here.
لێرەوە from here	من لێرەوە دێم. I am coming from here.
ئێرە ere	من دێمە ئێرە. /من دێم بۆ ئێرە. I am coming here.
لەوێ there	من لەوێم. I am there.
لەوێوە from there	دێم من لەوێوە. I am coming from there.
ئێوە there	من دێمە ئێوە / من دێم بۆ ئێوە. I am coming there.
لە پێشەوە in front	من لە پێشەوەم. I am in front.
لە پاشەوە behind	من لە پاشەوەم. I am behind.
لە ژێرەوە downstairs	من لە ژێرەوەم. I am downstairs.
لە ژوورەوە upstairs	من لە ژوورەوەم. I am upstairs.
لە دەرەوە outside	من لە دەرەوەم. I am outside.
لە دەرەوە from outside	من لە دەرەوە دێم. I am coming from outside.
دەرەوە outwards	من دێمە دەرەوە. /من دێم بۆ دەرەوە. I am coming out.
لە ناوەوەدا inside	من لە ناوەوەدام. I am inside.
لە ناوەوە from inside	من لە ناوەوە دێم. I come from inside.
ناوەوە inwards	من دێمە ناوەوە. /من دێم بۆ ناوەوە. I am coming inside.

PREPOSITIONS AND CIRCUMPOSITIONS

به with; by; to	من به هێمن دەڵێم. I'm telling **to** Hêmin. من به شەمەندەفەر دەچم I go **by** train. قاوەی به شیر دەخۆمەوە. I drink coffee **with** milk.		
به...دا through	من به دۆڵەکەدا دەچم. I go **through** the valley.		
به...ەوە on	وێنەیەک به دیوارەوەیە. A painting is **on** the wall.		
without, -less	بێکارم. I am jobless (unemployed).		
بێ، بەبێ، بەبێ...ئەوە	بێ تۆ ناڕۆم I am not going **without** you.		
بۆ for	This is **for** you. ئەمه بۆ تۆیە.		
لای next to	I am **next to** the tree. من لای دارەکەم.		
له in, at	له سلێمانی تۆ دەتبینم. I see you **in** Slemani. من له ماڵم. I am **at** home.		
له...ەوە from	من له هەولێرەوە دێم. I am coming **from** Hewlêr (Erbil). I am coming **from** home. من له ماڵەوە دێم.		
له...ەوە since; for	له سێ ساڵییەوە چاوەڕوانی تۆم. I have waited for you **for** three years.		
له بەر دا or له بەر in front of	من له بەر دەرگەی زانکۆم. I am **in front of** the university gate.		
له بن under	مکەدارە بن له من. I am **under** the tree.		
له بنەوە downstairs	I am **downstairs**. من له بنەوەم.		
له بانەوە upstairs	I am **upstairs**. من له بانەوەم.		
له... دا in, at	**in** my house له ماڵەکەمدا		

THE ADJECTIVES

سێوەکە لەناو قووتوودایە. The apple is **in** the box.		لەناو ...دا in (inside)	
خانوو لە نێوان دو داردایە. The house is **between** two trees.		لەنێو(ان ...)دا between	
من لە پشت دارەکەم. I am **behind** the tree.		لە پشت behind	
پێنووسەکە لەسەر مێزە. The pen is **on** the table. چۆلەکە لەسەر دارە. The bird is **above** the house.		لەسەر on, above	
من لەگەڵ تۆ دەڕۆم. I am going with you.		with (together) لەگەڵ، لەگەڵ ...دا	

THE ADJECTIVES

1. Adjective as a Modifier

In this case the substantive is determined by the adjective.

Words	Example	Meaning
باش - good مرۆڤ – person, people	مرۆڤی باش	good person
	هەندێ مرۆڤی باش	some good people
	مرۆڤێکی باش	a good person
	تۆ مرۆڤێکی باش دەبینیت.	You see a good person.

 *For further information see **Declension of nouns***

2. Adjective as an Adverb

Example	Meaning
تۆ جوان دیاری.	You look **beautiful**.
تۆ خێرا دەڕۆیت.	You are going **quickly/fast**.

3. Adjective as a Predicate with "to be"

Example	Meaning
تۆ باشیت.	You are **good**.
تۆ مرۆڤێکی باشیت.	You are a **good** person.
ئەو دوورە.	He/She/It is **far**.

4. Formation of Adjectives from Nouns

Noun	Adjective
بەرد (stone)	بەردی (stony)
تاوان (guilt)	تاوانبار (guilty)
ناو (name)	ناودار (famous)
زێڕ (gold)	زێڕین (golden)
هێز (power)	بەهێز (powerful)

5. Formation of Adjectives from Verbs (Participle)

Verb	Past Tense	Meaning
خەوتن	ژنە خەوتووەکە	the woman asleep
ڕۆیشتن	ژنە ڕۆیشتووەکە	the woman who has gone
فڕین	چۆلەگە فڕیوەکە	the bird that has flown

Verb	Suffix	Verb stem	Participle
برژاندن (to grill)	‑او	برژ‑	برژاو (grilled)
بردن (to take)	‑او	بر‑	براو (taken)
نووسین (to write)	‑راو	نووس‑	نووسراو (written)

THE ADJECTIVES

6. Substantiation of adjectives

Adjective	Example	Meaning
گەورە big/old	گەورەی ماڵ	the eldest (person) of the house
جوان beautiful	جوانەکەی شار	the most beautiful (person) in town
	جوانی	beauty

7. Comparative

Adjective	Comparative	Superlative
باش - good	تر- + Adjective	ترین- + Adjective
دوور - far	Example: باشتر (better) دوورتر (further)	Example: باشترین (the best) دوورترین (the furthest)

کەیوان لە بارام دوورترە.

(Saturn is further away than Mars.)

گەورەیی زەمین دو هێندەی بارامە.

(The Earth is twice as big as Mars.)

بارام بەقەت ئۆرانۆس گەورەیە.

(Mars is as big as Uranus.)

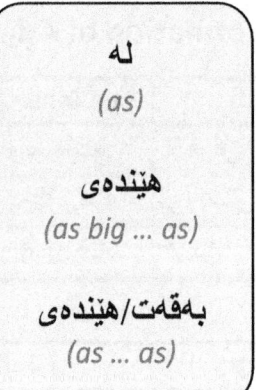

لە
(as)

هێندەی
(as big ... as)

بەقەت/هێندەی
(as ... as)

CONJUNCTIONS AND SUBORDINATE CLAUSES

Conjunctions in Sorani

In Sorani, as in all languages, the conjunctions are needed to introduce and connect main and subordinate clauses.

Conjunction	Example
و و or و and	من و تۆ دەتوانین بچین بۆ سینەما. I **and** you can go to the movies.
یان or	من سێوەکان یان هەرمێکان دەخۆم. I eat apples **or** pears.
یان ...یانیش either ... or	یان تۆ یانیش ئەو دەتوانێت بێت. **Either** you **or** he can come.
یش... یش as well as	منیش و هێمنیش سێو دەخۆین. I **and** Hêmin eat apples.
نە ... نە ـش neither... nor	من نە سێو و نە هەرمێش ناخۆم. I eat **neither** apples **nor** pears.
هەم... هەمیش both ... and	من سێویش و هەرمێ دەخۆم من هەم سێو و هەمیش هەرمێ دەخۆم. I eat **both** apples **and** pears.
بەڵام but	بەڵام من سێو ناخۆم. **But** I don't eat apples.
ئەگەر نا otherwise; or	تەلەفۆنم بۆ بکە، ئەگەر نا لە بیری دەکەم. Call me, **or** I'll forget it.
لەبەر ئەوەیە therefore, that's why	من دەڕۆم بۆ بەریتانیا، لە بەر ئەوەیە لێرەم. من دەڕۆمە بەریتانیا، لە بەر ئەوەیە لێرەم. I'm going to Britain, **that's why** I'm here.
بەهەرهاڵ after all, anyway	بە هەر هاڵ دەتوانم بخۆم. I can eat **anyway**.
دیسانەوە still	من دەتوانم دیسانەوە بخۆم. I can **still** eat.

CONJUNCTIONS AND SUBORDINATE CLAUSES

گەر/ئەگەر if	گەر بڕۆم، تەلەفۆنت بۆ دەکەم. If I go, I'll call you.		
هەر چەندە ...یش even though	هەر چەندە خواردیشم، کەچی هێشتا برسیمە. Even though I've eaten, I'm still hungry.		
کە that, thus, so that, so	من دەڵێم بۆ تۆ کە ئەوەی لێی تێبگەی. I say it so you understand.		
پێش ئەوەی before	پێش ئەوەی بڕۆم، ئەوم بینی. Before I left, I saw him.		
دوای ئەوەی after	دوای ئەوەی ڕۆشتم، ئەوم بینی. After I left, I saw him.		
چوونکە because	چوونکە ڕۆشتم، ئەوم بینی. Because I left, I saw him.		
کاتێک کە when	کاتێک کە ڕۆشتم، ئەوم بینی. When I left, I saw him.		
چۆن /هەر کە as soon as	هەر کە من گەیشتم، نان دەخۆین. As soon as I arrive, we'll eat.		
هەتا as long as	هەتا من لێرە بم، دەتوانی بخوێنیتەوە. As long as I'm here, you can read.		
لە بری/ لە ژیاتی (instead/in place of)	لە بری ئەوەی لەگەڵت بێم، لە ماڵ دەمێنمەوە. Instead of coming with you, I'm staying home.		

CONJUNCTIONS AND SUBORDINATE CLAUSES

Subordinate Clauses in Sorani

بیستم **که** لێم دەگەڕێی.
I heard (**that**) you were looking for me.

که هاتمەوە ماڵ خواردن دەخۆم.
When I get home, I'm going to eat.

دەخەوم **تاکو** بتوانم سبەی زوو هەڵسم
I'm going to sleep **so** I can get up early tomorrow.

ناتوانم بڕۆم، **چوونکه** نەخۆشم.
I can't go **because** I'm sick.

پێش ئەوەی بڕۆم، تەلەفۆنت بۆ دەکەم .
Before I go, I'll call you.

دوای ئەوەی هاتمەوە ماڵ، خواردنم خوارد.
After I came home, I ate.

ڕەنگه نەچم بۆ فەرەنسا، چونکە بلیتم نییە .
Maybe I can't go to France <u>because</u> I don't have a ticket.

ئەو کاتەی سەرم دەشووشت، دەنگی تەلەفۆن دەهات .
While I was showering, you could hear the phone.

ئەو کاتەی منی بینی، ڕووی خۆی گۆڕی .
When he saw me, he turned around.

هەتا سەرم شووشت، باوکم ڕۆیی .
By the time I showered, my father had left.

هەتا بمێنم، خۆشم دەوێی .
As long as I live, I will love you.

CONJUNCTIONS AND SUBORDINATE CLAUSES

چۆن تۆم بینی، خۆشم ویستی .
The moment I saw you, I fell in love with you.

لەگەڵ ئەوەی دوێنێ درەنگیش چوومەوە ماڵ، دایووبابم توورە نەبوون.
Although I went home late last night, my parents weren't mad.

من ئەوەم وت، بۆ ئەوەی بڕۆی.
I said that **to make** you leave.

ئێمە یەکتر دەناسین، بەڵام دیسانیش ناتوانم لێی بپرسم .
We know each other, but **still** I can't ask her.

بلێتەکەم هەڵوەشاوە، بۆیە ناچوومە هەولێر .
My ticket was cancelled, **so/that's why** I did not go to Erbil.

ئەگەر ئەمڕۆ درەنگ بچمەوە ماڵ، باوکم توورە دەبێت .
If I go home late tonight, my father will get mad.

خۆزگە پێشتر تۆم بناسیایە .
I wish I had met you earlier.

خۆزگە نەچوومبام...
If only I hadn't left...

خۆزگە لێرە بووینایە.
I wish we were there.

STRUCTURE OF THE SORANI VERBS
The Simple Verbs
Infinitive form of the Sorani verbs is formed by following six endings;
ـان- ،ـاندن- ،ـوون- ،ـدن- ،ـتن- ،ـین-

- گۆڕین ،نووسین ،بینین etc.
  The Conjugation in the Present Present/Future Tense is regular,
  e.g.: دەنووسم، دەبینم، دەگۆڕم، بنووسە!

- کردن ،چوون ،ۆتن ،ڕۆیشتن
  The Conjugation in the Present/Future Tense is irregular,
  e.g.: دەڕۆم، دەڵێم، دەچم، دەکەم، بڕۆ!

- بڕژاندن ،ڕووخاندن ،لکاندن
  The Conjugation in the Present Tense/Future has the same rule ا-
  becomes ێ, e.g.: دەڵکێنم، دەڕووخێنم، دەبڕژێنم

- کێشان ،پێوان ،هێنان   کۆڵان ،تۆران ،سوتان
  There are two possibilities of conjugation for the verbs with ان-
  1. ان- drops out, e.g.: دەهێنم، دەپێوم، بکێشە!
  2. ا- becomes ێ- e.g.: دەسووتێم، دەتۆرێم، دەکۆڵێم، بکۆڵێ!
  Exception: دان: دەدەم، بدە!

The Compound Verbs

- These verbs consist of a noun or adjective and a verb. These verbs are always written separately, except when the verb is nominal.
  چاک بوون، قسە کردن، غار دان، نەخۆش کەوتن، بڵاو کردنەوە
- In conjugation, the noun/adjective part remains the same and the verb is conjugated.

من قسەم دەکرد.	من قسەم کرد.	من قسە دەکەم.
I was talking.	I talked.	I talk.
من غارم دەدا.	من غارم دا.	من غار دەدەم.
I was running.	I ran.	I run.

STRUCTURE OF THE SORANI VERBS | 86

The Separable Compound Verbs

If verbs with prepositions like بە or لە stand with a pronoun, the pronoun merges with the vowel of the preposition to form ‍ـێ.

پرسین لێ (to ask somebody)

I ask you.	من **لێت** دەپرسم. ← من لە تۆ دەپرسم.
I ask him/her.	من **لێی** دەپرسم. ← من لە ئەو دەپرسم.
I ask us.	من **لێمان** دەپرسم. ← من لە ئێمە دەپرسم.
I ask you.	من **لێتان** دەپرسم. ← من لە ئێوە دەپرسم.
I ask them.	من **لێیان** دەپرسم ← من لە ئەوان دەپرسم.

پێ وتن (to tell somebody)

I tell you.	من **پێت** دەڵێم. ← من بە تۆ دەڵێم.
I tell him/her.	من **پێی** دەڵێم. ← من بە ئەو دەڵێم.
I tell us.	من **پێمان** دەڵێم. ← من بە ئێمە دەڵێم.
I tell you.	من **پێتان** دەڵێم. ← من بە ئێوە دەڵێم.
I tell them.	من **پێیان** دەڵێم. ← من بە ئەوان دەڵێم.

The Separable Verbs

Prefix	Compound verbs & the Conjugation in the Present	Conjugation in the Past Tense
دا-	دانیشتن، داکەوتن، داهێنان من دادەنیشم – I'm sitting	من دانیشتم I sat
دەر-	دەرکەوتن، دەرهێنان، دەرچوون من دەردەکەوم - I go out	من دەرکەوتم I went out
هەڵ-	هەڵهاتن، هەڵستان، هەڵقوڵان من هەڵدەستم - I stand up	من هەڵسام I stood up
لێ-	لێکردن، لێخستن، لێخوورین من لێدەخوورم - I drive	من لێخووریم I drove
پێ-	پێکەنین، پێدان من پێدەکەنم - I laugh	من پێکەنیم I laughed
پێک-	پێککردن، پێکهێنان من پێکدەهێنم - I'm creating	من پێکمهێنا I created
را-	ڕێنڕاپە، ڕاپرسین، ڕاهێنان من ڕادەهێنم - I'm training	من ڕامهێنا I trained
ڕێک-	ڕێکخستن، ڕێککەوتن، ڕێکپۆشین من ڕێکدەخەم - I organize	من ڕێکمخست I organized
تێ-	تێپەڕین، تێکۆشین، تێکەوتن من تێدەکۆشم - I struggle	من تێکۆشیم I struggled
تێک-	تێکدان، تێکخستن، تێکچوون ئەو تێکدەچێت - He/She's losing	ئەو تێکچوو He/She lost
Suffix		
-ەوە	گەڕانەوە، بینینەوە، کردنەوە دەگەڕێمەوە - I return	من گەڕامەوە I returned

 Intransitive verbs *are not being separated in the past tenses.*

THE NUMBERS

Cardinal Numbers

سفر 0 ۰	ده 10 ۱۰	بیست 20 ۲۰	سی 30 ۳۰
یەک 1 ۱	یانزه 11 ۱۱	بیست و یەک 21 ۲۱	چل 40 ٤۰
دوو 2 ۲	دوانزه 12 ۱۲	بیست و دوو 22 ۲۲	پەنجا 50 ٥۰
سێ 3 ۳	سیانزه 13 ۱۳	بیست و سێ 23 ۲۳	شەست 60 ٦۰
چوار 4 ٤	چوارده 14 ۱٤	بیست و چوار 24 ۲٤	حەفتا 70 ۷۰
پێنج 5 ٥	پانزه 15 ۱٥	بیست و پێنج 25 ۲٥	هەشتا 80 ۸۰
شەش 6 ٦	شانزه 16 ۱٦	بیست شەش 26 ۲٦	نەوەت 90 ۹۰
حەوت 7 ۷	حەڤده 17 ۱۷	بیست و حەوت 27 ۲۷	سەد 100 ۱۰۰
هەشت 8 ۸	هەژده 18 ۱۸	بیست و هەشت 28 ۲۸	هەزار 1000 ۱۰۰۰
نۆ 9 ۹	نۆزده 19 ۱۹	بیست و نۆ 29 ۲۹	سەد هەزار 100.000 ۱۰۰۰۰۰
ملیۆن 1.000.000 ۱۰۰۰۰۰۰		ملیار 1.000.000.000 ۱۰۰۰۰۰۰۰۰۰	
هەزار و نۆ سەد و نەوەت و نۆ 1999 ۱۹۹۹			
دو هەزار و نۆزده 2019 ۲۰۱۹			

Writing of the date

Ordinal Numbers	Fractions	Iterative number جار word
1. يەكەم	1/2 نيو	جارێک – once
2. دووەم	1/3 لە سێیان یەک	دوو جار – twice
3. سێیەم	1/4 لە چواران یەک چارێک	سێ جار – thrice
21. بیست و یەكەم	10/100 لە سەدان دە	۲۱ جار – m21 times
34. سی و چوارەم	3/10 لە دەیان سێ	جار ۱۰۰ – 100 times

Writing of the date

Sorani		English
ی ۱ ی نیسان	یەكی نیسان	1st of April
٥ ی گوڵان	پێنجی گوڵان	5th of May
ی ۲٥ ی گوڵان	بیست و پێنجی گوڵان	25th of May
	لە ۱ ی نیساندا	on 1st of April
	لە ٥ ی گوڵاندا	on 5th of May
	لە ۲٥ ی گوڵاندا	on 25th of May
	لە ۱۹۹۰ دا	in 1990
	لە گوڵانی ۱۹۹۰ دا	in May 1990
	بیست و یەكی گوڵانی دو هەزار و هەژدەیان	21.05.2018

VERB STEMS

Verb (intransitive)	Present stem	Past stem
بارین (to rain)	‑بار‑	باری‑
چوون (to go)	‑چ‑	چوو‑
دانیشتن (to sit (down))	‑دانیش‑ دادەنیشم	دانیشت‑ دادەنیشتم دانەنیشتم
دەرباز بوون (to pass (by))	دەرباز ‑ب‑ دەرباز دەبم	دەرباز بوو‑ دەرباز بووم
دەرچوون (to go out)	دەر‑چ‑	دەرچوو‑
فڕین (to fly)	‑فڕ‑	فڕی‑
گەڕانەوە (to return)	گەڕێ‑..‑ەوە	گەڕا‑ەوە
گەڕین (to travel)	‑گەڕ‑	گەڕی‑
گەیشتن (to arrive)	‑گەیش‑	گەیشت‑
گۆڕین (to change)	‑گۆڕ‑	گۆڕی‑
هاتن (to come)	دێم ‑ێ‑	هات‑
هەڵهاتن (to escape/run)	هەڵ‑هێ‑	هەڵهات‑
هەڵقوڵان (to flow)	هەڵ‑قوڵ‑	هەڵقوڵا‑
هەڵستان (to stand up)	هەڵ‑ست‑ or هەڵ‑س‑	هەڵسا‑
ژین (to live)	‑ژی‑	ژیا‑
کەوتن (to fall)	‑کەو‑	کەوت‑
کۆخین (to caugh)	‑کۆخ‑	کۆخی‑
کوڵان (to cook)	‑کوڵێ‑	کوڵا‑
مان (to stay/remain)	‑مێن‑	ما‑
مردن (to die)	‑مر‑	مرد‑
نوین/نوستن (to sleep)	‑نو‑	‑نویی‑/‑نوست‑

VERB STEMS

Verb	Present stem	Past stem
پێکەنین (to laugh)	‑پێ‑کەن‑	‑پێکەنی‑
ڕۆیشتن (to go)	‑ڕۆ‑	‑ڕۆیشت‑
سڕ بوون (to be cold)	‑سڕ‑ب‑	سڕ بوو‑
سوورانەوە (to turn)	‑سووریٚ‑...‑ەوە	سوورا‑...‑ەوە
سووتان (to burn)	‑سووتێ‑	‑سووتا‑
تەواو بوون (to end)	‑تەواو‑ب‑	تەواو بوو‑
تێپەڕین (to pass (by))	‑تێ‑پەڕ‑	تێپەڕی‑
تۆڕان (to sulk)	‑تۆڕێ‑	‑تۆڕا‑
خەوتن (to sleep)	‑خەو‑	‑خەوت‑
زیز بوون (to sulk)	زیز‑ب‑	زیز بوو‑

Verb (transitive)	Present stem	Past stem
بەردان (to let)	بەر‑دە‑	بەر‑دا
بردن (to take)	‑بە‑	‑برد‑
برژاندن (to grill)	‑برژێن‑	‑برژاند‑
بینین (to see)	‑بین‑	‑بینی‑
چێس کردن (to finish)	چێس‑کە‑	چێس‑کرد
دان (to give)	‑دە‑	‑دا‑
دەرهێنان (to publish)	دەر‑هێن‑	دەر هێنا
دیار کردن (to show)	دیار‑کە‑ / دیار دەکەم	دیار‑کرد / دیارم کرد
دۆزینەوە (to find)	دۆز‑...‑ەوە / دەدۆزمەوە	دۆزی‑...‑ەوە / دۆزیمەوە
دوورین (to sew)	‑دوور‑	‑دووری‑
فرۆشتن (to sell)	‑فرۆش‑	‑فرۆشت‑
گەڕاندن (to set/rotate)	‑گەڕێن‑	‑گەڕاند‑
گرتن (to catch)	‑گر‑	‑گرت‑

VERB STEMS

گۆڕان (to change)	ـگۆڕێـ	ـگۆڕاـ
گوزەر کردن (to pass (by))	گوزەر ـکەـ	گوزەر ـکردـ
هاوێشتن (to throw straight)	ـهاوێژـ	ـهاوێشتیـ
هەڵگرتن (to lift up)	ـهەڵـگرـ	ـهەڵـگرتـ
هەول دان (to try)	هەول ـدەـ	هەول ـداـ
هێنان (to bring)	ـهێنـ	ـهێناـ
ئیش کردن (to work)	ئیش ـکەـ	ئیش ـکردـ
ژماردن (to count)	ـژمێرـ	ـژماردـ
کردن (to do/make)	ـکەـ	ـکردـ
کردنەوە (to open)	ـکە...ـئەوەـ	کردـ...ـەوە
کڕین (to buy)	ـکڕـ	ـکڕیـ
لە بیر کردن (to forget)	لە بیر ـکەـ	لە بیر ـکردـ
لێخوورین (to drive/ride)	لێـخوورـ	لێ خووری
مووشین (to throw)	ـمووشـ	ـمووشیـ
ناردن (to send)	ـنێرـ	ـناردـ
ناسین (to know sb./smt.)	ـناسـ	ـناسیـ
نووسین (to write)	ـنووسـ	ـنووسیـ
پاراستن (to protect)	ـپارێزـ	ـپاراستـ
پەنهان کردن (to hide)	پەنهان ـکەـ	پەنهان ـکردـ
پەرش کردن (to publish)	پەرش ـکەـ	پەرش ـکردـ
پێوان (to measure)	ـپێوـ	ـپێواـ
پچراندن (to separate)	ـپچرێنـ	ـپچراندـ
پرسین (to ask)	ـپرسـ	ـپرسیـ
پساندن (to separate)	ـپسێنـ	ـپساندـ
قسە کردن (to speak)	قسە ـکەـ	قسە ـکردـ
راهێنان (to train)	ـراـهێنـ	راـهێنا
راکردن (to run)	ـراـکەـ	راـکردـ

رازاندنەوە (to decorate)	رازێن...-ەوە	رازاند...ئەوە
ڕێکخستن (to organize)	ڕێک-خە-	-ڕێکخست-
ڕوانین (to look at/watch)	-ڕوان-	-ڕوانی-
سەما کردن (to dance)	سەما-کە-	سەما-کرد
سەیر کردن (to look at)	سەیر-کە-	سەیر-کرد
ساز کردن (to do/make smt.)	ساز-کە-	ساز-کرد
شاردنەوە (to hide)	شار-...-ەوە	شارد-...-ەوە
شۆرین (to wash)	-شۆر-	-شۆری-
شوشتن (to wash)	-شۆ-	-شوشت-
تەماشە کردن (to watch)	تەماشە-کە-	تەماشە-کرد
تەواو کردن (to finish)	تەواو-کە-	تەواو-کرد
توانین (can)	-توان-	-توانی-
وەڵام دانەوە (to answer)	وەڵام-دە-ەوە	وەڵام-داوە
وتن (to say)	-ڵێ-	-وت-
غار دان (to run)	غار-دە-	غار-دا
خاوێن کردنەوە (to clean)	خاوێن کە-ەوە	خاوێن-کردەوە
خەلاس کردن (to finish)	خەلاس کە-	خەلاس-کرد
خواردن (to eat)	-خۆ-	-خوارد-
خواردنەوە (to drink)	خۆ-...-ەوە	خوارد-...-ەوە
خواستن (to want)	-خواز-	-خواست-
خوێندن (to study)	-خوێن-	-خوێند-
خوێندنەوە (to read)	خوێن-...-ەوە	خوێند-...-ەوە
یاری کردن (to play)	یاری-کە-	یاری-کرد
زانین (to know)	-زان-	-زانی-

The Abbreviations

isol. – isolated
P. ending – Personal ending
Pl. – plural
sb. – somebody

Sg. – singular
sth. – something

Printed in Great Britain
by Amazon